CHESAPEAKE
BOYHOOD

CHESAPEAKE

Memoirs of a Farm Boy

BOYHOOD

WILLIAM H. TURNER

Illustrations by the author

THE JOHNS HOPKINS UNIVERSITY PRESS
BALTIMORE AND LONDON

All photographs are by William H. Turner except as noted.
Photograph of Robert H. Rockwell courtesy of American Museum of Natural
History Library.

Designed by William H. Turner
Mel Baughman, Publishing Consultant

First published as *Memoirs of a Farm Boy* in 1995 by Turner Press, Onley, Virginia
Johns Hopkins Paperbacks edition, 1997
06 05 04 03 02 01 00 99 98 97   5 4 3 2 1

The Johns Hopkins University Press
2715 North Charles Street
Baltimore, Maryland 21218-4319
The Johns Hopkins Press Ltd., London

Library of Congress Cataloging-in-Publication Data

Turner, William H. (William Henry), 1935–
  [Memoirs of a farm boy]
  Chesapeake boyhood : memoirs of a farm boy / William H. Turner.
      p.   cm.—(Maryland paperback bookshelf)
  Originally published: Memoirs of a farm boy. Onley, Va. : Turner Press, 1995.
  ISBN 0-8018-5589-6 (pbk. : alk. paper)
    1. Turner, William H. (William Henry), 1935– —Childhood and youth.
2. Farm life—Chesapeake Bay Region (Md. and Va.)   3. Farm life—Eastern Shore
(Md. and Va.)   4. Chesapeake Bay Region (Md. and Va.—Biography.   5. Eastern
Shore (Md. and Va.—Biography.   6. Hunting—Anecdotes.   7. Fishing—Anecdotes.
I. Title.   II. Series.
CT275.T955A3   1997
975.5´18—dc21   96-45129
                                                                              CIP

A catalog record for this book is available from the British Library.

In Memory Of
My Parents

Nellie Custis Turner
(1911 - 1995)

Major Evans Turner
(1911 - 1991)

CONTENTS

PREFACE

This book is quite likely an offshoot or by-product of a newsletter called <u>Tracks</u> which I write for Turner Sculpture, a company owned by my son David and myself. This facility, a combination of gallery, studio and foundry, casts and markets our bronze sculpture. When I say likely, I do not mean to be vague or elusive. Some ideas come to me so subconsciously and insidiously that I really forget how or when they started. Then there are times when an idea comes as instantly and clearly as the proverbial light bulb. This book is a product of the former process.

In <u>Tracks</u>, I began many issues ago to narrate our company history. However, this soon took on an autobiographical format involving many of my childhood friends and my experiences with them. Many of these experiences were a little lengthy for a newsletter and, if published serially on a quarterly basis, I thought that one may have had trouble picking up the thread of a story after three months. However, from the beginning, I received a great deal of encouragement from my readers and many said I should write a book. So I did.

In my early years I was an avid hunter. I derived great pleasure from this and helped feed lots of people. Though the smell of wet duck feathers and burned gunpowder still brings back many happy memories, I find it difficult to kill anything anymore, even going to the extreme of taking ants and beetles out of the fireplace before the flames consume them. Perhaps this is because I now make a living recreating life in sculpture, not destroying it.

You may detect this old love of the chase in some of my stories. I hope you also note that what I considered important was not how many birds were shot nor the type of gun used, but the people who participated, what they said, how they felt about things, and how life was changing as these things happened (as it certainly continues to do).

Except for the beginning and the end, there is no chronological order to this book. This is because at times the main subject may be people, and elsewhere it may be rural life in general, or places. In covering one subject I may relate happenings over a length of time in which various people were involved at different periods and in different pursuits.

I have done no research while writing this book, only referring to my own notes, which I started keeping at age twelve. Observations that I have made on nature, etc., may or may not be accurate; however, I believe what I have written, or what some of my old friends have told me that they believed. I did not want this book to be the product of someone else's labor in any way. This is the philosophy I used to a certain extent in building boats and which I apply to a large extent in my sculpture.

The drawings could have been better done by others, but following the same logic, I did these also. For good or bad or perhaps some of each, it is my book.

All the people are real and all the events are true. It's not that I am so honest that I cannot lie. It's just that I lack the imagination to fabricate.

For most of you, this book might seem to be about ordinary people in ordinary times. But the people I write about here were heroes in my eyes because they were friends of mine. The times are special because it was my growing-up time, the only one I ever had. It is also about nature and how these people interacted with it, loved it, preyed upon it, and felt about it.

Many of the characters I've written about are now gone and it seems to me that these types do not appear on life's scene any more (at least not characters of that stature). To me they were not just friends but teachers and veritable giants in the art of country living. I suspect that my admiration for and association with them during my impressionable years may magnify their importance to some extent, but they deserve remembrance.

Some of the controversial events described in this book occurred because of innocence and/or necessity. The fact that I describe them does not mean that I now approve of what occurred. Actually, I cannot tell many of the more interesting things because of the statute of limitations, revenge, embarrassment to the living, etc.

The world is changing rapidly in rural areas. Many activities encouraged and demanded by the environment and the existing technology of a generation or two ago are not exactly state-of-the-art now, nor proper, considering changing values.

And then there is the time/distance factor which causes the past to seem so much more interesting than the present. This factor is always there, and I vividly remember my late friend and teacher, Mitt Bundick, telling me about the myriad shore birds and waterfowl in the days of his youth and Robert Rockwell telling of Africa and Alaska as they used to be.

Much decline in the world's quality of life is directly related to the increase in human population and a decrease in wildlife habitat. The ducks and geese are not nearly so plentiful now. No longer can you take a bushel basket to any saltwater shoreline and fill it with large *bull-tongue* oysters in a few minutes. The worst change though, has been in the minds of the people (including myself). There was a time when property lines were unimportant except in planting a field or cutting timber. One could take his hounds and chase raccoons or foxes almost anywhere with no restrictions; no one minded if you helped yourself to oysters, and POSTED signs were rare. Now people are very conscious of property lines and very careful about who may come into their domain.

Actually, the population in Accomack and Northampton Counties, which make up the geographically-isolated part of Virginia known as the Eastern Shore, my home, has decreased since the turn of the century. So it is not the numbers that have caused change, it is technology that has altered our lifestyle. Fifty years ago every little subsistence farm (there were few big ones) supported several large families: the owner and his tenants, field hands, or sharecroppers. But these people did not all own several cars, did not poison the land and eventually the Bay, with chemicals, and did not throw plastic refuse along the highways. People were, in those days, much more inconspicuous and less lethal. Instead of motoring out to the shopping centers several times a week with a credit card and stopping by a fast-food place on the way home and tossing the trash out the window, visits to the store were once-a-week rituals, eagerly anticipated by the entire family. Depending on the season, purchases were paid for in cash, eggs, or simply 'put on the books' until the next harvest.

These stores were general in every sense of the word. In one stop a person could get rid of eggs, buy a shotgun, rope, nails, ginger snaps, salt, sugar or whatever else one needed, which was not much. They were communication centers where all the news was heard and told. Finally, they were entertainment centers, especially for the men where, more or less, innocent games of chance were played.

Except for lime, chemicals were almost unknown. We squashed crop-eating bugs between the index finger and the thumb, and weeds were hoed and pulled by hand. Manure from the livestock was used on the fields instead of commercial fertilizer. Paper bags, Kraft wrapping paper, and string were never discarded but used repeatedly until they just biologically degraded.

There was a certain closeness to the earth and its

products and a satisfaction in living that cannot now be duplicated either physically or mentally. It is history. So what I have tried to do in this book is describe not only the physical and cultural aspect of rural life forty to fifty years ago but also to mirror the character of a few local people and the environment which contributed to my life.

ACKNOWLEDGMENTS

Several people have helped me in this book in various ways. Some refreshed my memory, some helped in my grammar and speling and some were professional writers who offered encouragement.

They are listed in alphabetical order, a wonderful invention in cases like this.

Becky Ashby

Curtis Badger

Mel Baughman

Thane Bierwert

Dorothy Blair

Joe Carruthers

Clayton Cisar*

Winter Cullen, III

Major Robertson Doughty, III**

Jackie Duer

Norvin Hagan

John Hamberger

Claribel Hargis

Robert Hutchinson

Nancy Irvin

Ronnie Kellam

Alfred Mapp

Tom Nicholson

William Nicholson

Lucian Niemeyer

Helen Northam

Robert Pase

Lloyd Proctor

Thelma Schaufler

Nancy Schiffer

Franky Smith

Ida Sorensen

Drew Steis

Mary Ann Turner

Kate Wallace

Paul Wirth

*(1936 - 1991) Clayton worked for the United States government. He once expropriated a whole box of ledger books for my note taking.

**(1935 - 1953) Bobby was killed only two weeks before high school graduation. I used one of his decoys as a model for the drawing on page 103.

"Within is a country that may have the prerogative over the most pleasant places knowne, for large and pleasant navigable Rivers, heaven & earth never agreed better to frame a place for man's habitation..."

CAPTAIN JOHN SMITH

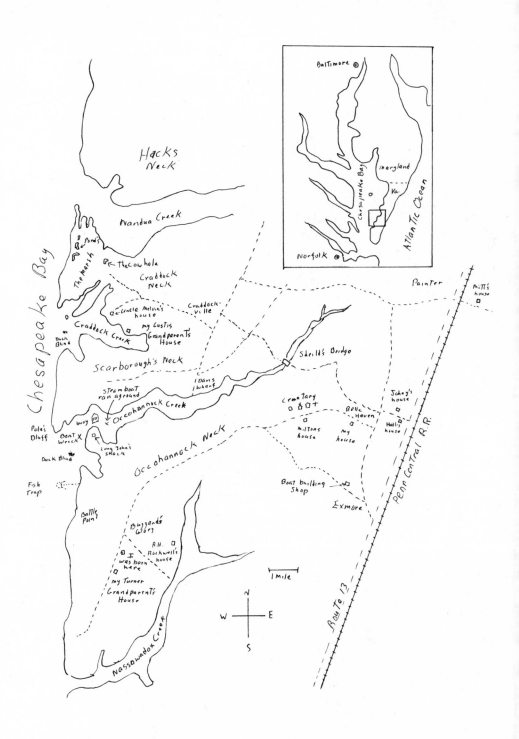

IN THE BEGINNING

*"All men of whatsoever quality they be, who have done anything of excellence,
or which may properly resemble excellence, ought, if they are persons of truth
and honesty, to describe their life with their own hand. . . "*

Benvenuto Cellini

To be truthful, Buzzards' Glory, later known as
Persimmon Tree, was not a town or even a village. It was
merely a vague, ill-defined area where one dirt road inter-
cepted another. These dirt roads were formerly just wagon
tracks and, before that, Indian paths. There were two grocery
stores in this area, a part-time barber, a church, and about ten
houses within a five hundred yard radius of the meeting of the
two roads. That was it.

It was in Buzzards' Glory, Virginia, that I was born on
May 27, 1935. (Buzzards' Glory is one mile west of Jamesville. There is a post office in Jamesville, and I sometimes
use that address as my birthplace when I want to impress
someone.) My mother, Nellie Custis Turner, loved to pick
strawberries, and May is strawberry season in Virginia. She
picked berries until the day I was born, so I was, for awhile,
known as the 'strawberry baby'.

When I probe the utmost recesses of my mind, trying
to find my earliest impressions and memories of life, the first
images that insidiously come include standing beside my

1

mother in a strawberry patch, cold dew on the foliage, and finding a cottontail's nest nestled in the weeds and berry leaves, replete with a lining of rabbit hair, dry grass, and young cottontails with unopened eyes.

Throughout her life, picking berries was one of my mother's few pleasures, though it was a form of work. As you probably have guessed, I cannot see a strawberry today that I do not think of these things and my mother working in the fields over a half century ago. Simultaneously, I recall her last intelligible words a few years ago before Alzheimer's disease cruelly and slowly extinguished her bright and beautiful mind: "I've worked all my life to pay for my home and now I have this mental disease."

We lived on a farm in this area for about five years, and it was here that I first came into contact with certain factors which helped shape my career as a sculptor. When I was about three years old, I first encountered clay. My father had dug a hole for a new one-seater outhouse, and I walked through this red mud, leaving well-defined footprints. It was fun to push it around with my hands to form some kind of shape and later let it harden in the sun.

Very early on, I was encouraged to work with my hands, and I have done so all my life. (I hear there is money in working with your head, and someday I am going to try that.) My father was a carpenter and a farmer, his father a blacksmith and a barrel maker and a farmer. My other grandfather was a farmer. One of my great-grandfathers was also a blacksmith. Another was a ship's captain. I have inherited the influence of the earth, the sea, fire and metal.

Life in Buzzards' Glory was simple, yet rich and satisfying. Everything related to the Chesapeake Bay and the soil and one's sweat. Wildlife and domestic animals were abundant in those unmechanized subsistence-farming days, and our lives were very closely geared to the environment.

One of the first animals I owned was a pet duck, an Easter present. I was very upset when it later appeared on the supper table, head and feet missing, lying on its back with legs in the air. However, just as in Port Royal, Lake Forest, Greenwich, Palm Beach, Hobe Sound, and other places that we have come to know, life in Buzzards' Glory also had its up side. My father once brought home a whole stalk of bananas, purchased at a Philadelphia farmers' market when he went there in the family truck to take some farm produce. I'd always wanted a banana! Now there was a whole stalk of them hanging in the shade in our chicken house.

The next animal that I remember owning, after the demise of my pet duck, was a dog for which I chose the unique name of Spot, partly because he had a spot. He also suffered a violent death. (We did not eat him; he was run over by a fish wagon.) I was told that he ran away to chase rabbits, but this did not lessen my grief. From then on, whenever we were riding in the family truck and came to a stop sign, the letters in STOP reminded me of my dog SPOT. Fortunately, there were very few stop signs in this part of Virginia, and we only went to town once a week.

Starting in early spring, about the same time the first osprey arrived, fish wagons would patrol the back roads peddling freshly-caught fish from the Chesapeake and its adjoining inlets, which we called creeks. Usually these fish wagons were small trucks or old converted autos with large boxes built into them to hold ice and fish.

The sight of so many different kinds of fish of various shapes and colors fascinated me. I recall that for twenty-five cents my mother could have three huge sea trout or croakers (an important eastern Atlantic food fish) thrown into her tin basin and a little butterfish as a bonus for me. I spent hours sitting next to the dirt road in front of our house listening for the mouth-blown horn announcing the approach of the fish wagon.

Living next to my paternal grandparents enriched my childhood, leaving me with many fond memories of them. My grandmother helped me pick wild flowers and taught me to hear the ocean in a conch shell. The first metalwork I ever witnessed was my grandfather's beating out shoes for his mules on an anvil. He had bought this anvil second-hand from my maternal great-grandfather, who was a wheelwright and blacksmith. It is now one of my most cherished possessions and was one of my major inheritances.

Easiest to recall were the smells: smells of sweating mules, coal in the blacksmith shop, and the appetizing aromas of my grandmother's pantry and kitchen. One cannot sculpt smells or paint them, and I suppose this is why nature gives them a special impact which makes them outlast the harvests of all the other senses.

The changing seasons always fascinated me, as I suppose is the case with all two-to-five-year olds. I could tell when it was spring because my mother took away my shoes and the fish wagons came. And when she gave my shoes back and I could hear hounds barking and the hogs were killed, I knew it was fall.

Buzzards' Glory was a paradise, but it also had another, darker side. I recall lying awake at night after hearing the chickens scream when some person, not as rich as I, stole a bird for the pot. Occasionally, a ham would be missing from the smokehouse. These episodes added a touch of excitement and no one became too upset. Seldom was more than one item taken. The sad aspect of this is that there was always someone who had a desperate need.

We had a neighbor called Aunt Lou who took advantage of the untimely death of one of my mother's chickens which had been run over by a Model T. Aunt Lou came over to ask if she could have this traffic victim. Now that had to be an unlucky or sick chicken to get run over on a dirt road where heavy traffic was two or three vehicles per day going at a clip of fifteen to twenty miles per hour. Everyone had a way of surviving!

Occasionally the outside world affected us. I witnessed my first blimp from a potato field, and once an airplane crashed in the nearby woods. This was an important event, and hundreds of people came in their horse carts, trucks, cars, and on foot to see it. I remember visiting the site with my father and bringing home a little twisted piece of aluminum, the first I had ever seen, so much lighter than a plow point!

The big intellectual event in my life at Buzzards' Glory occurred twice a year, in the spring and fall, when the new issues of the Sears & Roebuck and Montgomery Ward catalogs arrived. Immediately the old issues went to the outhouse and the new ones were placed in the library where I could look at the wares of the season: hardware, tools, clothes (which did not interest me much), duck decoys, rope, anchors, horse collars, bridles, shotguns, shells, outboard motors, etc.

Next in importance of time-reckoning events was the appearance of a black bear right in downtown Buzzards' Glory. This was the first creature of this kind to be seen on the Eastern Shore of Virginia since the 18th century.*

It all started, so they say, when the Chesapeake Bay froze over solid the previous year (about 1938 or 1939). This

---

* I have recently been told that there was a sighting in 1950.

gave the Eastern Shore a physical link with the western shore (notice the lack of capitals) for the first time in recorded history.* The erudites of Buzzards' Glory suggested that the bear traversed the Bay on the ice, but I now doubt that.

The honor of the first person to see this live bear went to Major Evans Turner, my father. It occurred one evening as he and I were walking home from the country store, which was about a quarter mile down the dirt road that passed in front of our house (a main artery, I suppose you would say).

We had spent an hour or so in the store, with my father proudly showing off his three-year-old son who would someday write books and design sculpture. As the evening light began to fade, we were heading home, perhaps with a small piece of rat cheese, some molasses in a jar, a piece of delicious salted 'heck' fish (haddock), or some ginger snaps. We were about half way home, and I was struggling to keep up with my father's long strides, when suddenly he halted. At first I thought he was waiting for me but when I caught up with him, he picked me up on his shoulders and pointed across the field to the edge of the woods behind one-legged Al Summers' house. Then he said to me, "There's a bear!" He pointed it out to me as fathers have done for sons since human beginnings, and finally, with my untrained eye, I discerned an object that looked like a large black shaggy dog standing on its hind legs next to a single bottom plow left in the field.

Gradually it grew darker, and after a few minutes we lost sight of the animal and continued home. By this time I was thoroughly frightened and insisted that my father carry me. We hurried to tell my mother about this extraordinary event. Before complete darkness, my father took some precautionary measures with a pig which we were fattening for

---

* The second time the two shores were connected was on April 15, 1964, when the Chesapeake Bay Bridge-Tunnel was completed. Since then, we have been forcibly linked to the insignificant rest of Virginia.

the winter and with our other livestock. There was a great deal of apprehension in our home that night, but nothing happened.

The following day my father told the story to everyone he saw, and he realized that many doubted him. He hoped someone else would see this strange animal to corroborate his story. Sometime in the next few days, my cousin (with the unique appellation of Johnny Smith) and I went to play near the edge of the woods, and we both caught a fleeting glimpse of a shaggy black form. I say "fleeting" because that is what we were doing after this momentary sighting, but an indelible image of this beast was imprinted on my brain. Of course, we knew instantly that it was no 'possum, squirrel, 'coon, or rabbit, which to that date was our lifetime list of animal sightings. It was huge, black and hairy, standing on its rear legs glaring down on us with beady, bloodshot, evil eyes. Saliva was dripping from its open maw in great globules, between long sharp teeth, apparently stimulated by thoughts of tender boys.

The steps to Johnny's grandmother's back porch were tall, and he still insists that each of us touched only two of the ten or so on our retreat to safety. We, of course, told our story, but everyone thought that we were victims of our imaginations.

That evening my father heard a commotion in the barnyard. The chickens squawked and the pig squealed, so he went to the back door and fired his shotgun into the air. All was quiet for the rest of the night.

The next morning my father went out to see whether or not our pig, supposed to sustain us through the winter, was still living. There was no damage to any of our livestock, but there were deep claw marks on the side of our corn stack, and my father was delighted to discover distinct bear tracks next to it. He put bushel baskets over all the tracks he could find to preserve them (and his reputation). As the day went by, the story got around that there really was some kind of unusual animal in Buzzards' Glory. The men decided that the time had come for the first bear hunt on the Eastern Shore in more than a century. As light began to fade, all the local hunters began to congregate in our barnyard with their coonhounds. Even Uncle Melvin Drummond came from Craddock Neck with his renowned pack. The hounds were turned loose, and the cold track began to get warmer and finally hot as they bore down on the prey, but the baying hounds faded into the distance, and it was literally days before some of them returned home. No one in our area ever saw the bear again. A few nights later we did hear that, many miles away, someone's pig was killed and partially eaten. I felt deeply sorry for those folks who would be eating no scrapple and sausage that winter.

Everything, including the Depression, was about three years late in getting to our part of the country; it finally caught up with us though, and we had to move. If, however, I am to continue receiving pies and cakes from her, I must first mention the birth, at Buzzards' Glory, of my sister. Of course, I cannot tell you the year.

EARLY ENTERPRISE

"A man who dares waste one hour of his time has not discovered the value of life."

Charles Darwin

I suppose that all youngsters at some time early in their lives contemplate an enterprise that will earn them a little money. The exception, of course, are the pampered brats born into the world worth many millions before the umbilical cord is cut and upon death being worth only a million or so, and eulogized for their contribution to the world as great persons. I should not be so harsh. It is certainly not their fault they were so unlucky as to not have to work for a living. The point of this story, however, is not to criticize the unfortunate but merely to relate a tale.

Early on in life, I got into bartering. For everyone, this was an important part of getting along in the country. Much of the bartering was done at the local store. Pop bottles that I turned in for a one-cent deposit were my first items of trade. Once I found four in one week.

My economy got a big boost when I inherited what would compare to a counterfeiting machine. My Aunt Noah left me an old hen which turned out to be a good layer. I would sit for hours in the hen house waiting for nature to take its course so I could run to the store to trade an egg for a piece of candy. Being an early victim of my biological drives, I never saved the eggs, and this kept me from getting a new two-cent candy bar that whetted my appetite every time I saw it.

Then came the day when I ran my hand under my hen and there were two eggs instead of one. I immediately grasped one in each hand and headed for the store and the two-cent candy bar. The trip was about a quarter-mile, and I was so eager to get there that I took a short cut. Normally, I walked along the dirt road, but this time I headed directly across our potato field, which my father had asked me to avoid. There was a ditch at the edge of the field where it bordered on the dirt road, and this was my only obstacle. I was running as fast as I could and decided to jump the ditch. I gauged my steps as carefully as an Olympic broad jumper and lifted off at the last instant. I didn't get very far however, because a bit of blackberry vine caught my foot, and I went egg first into the bottom of the ditch. I was only scratched up a little bit, but both eggs were broken. There would be no new candy bar.

To make a sad story sadder, about two days later my old hen died. I suppose she sensed her demise and tried to unload her assets when she could.

My first real enterprise was as a salesman. Since I have already described Buzzards' Glory, and if you are versed in the great metropolitan art of sales, you will recognize immediately the demographic limitations which faced me at the tender age of four at the interception of Occohannock Neck Road and Salt Works Road. (All salesmen will, I am sure, quickly note the difference between an interception and an intersection as far as sales potential goes.)

However, I had a goal. I had seen an ad in <u>Grit</u> magazine showing a cowboy suit which I really wanted. The catch was that, to get this wardrobe, I must sell a set number of flower-seed packets and send the money off to a far-away city. I learned this only after my parents had explained it to me. In looking back, one must admire the trust of the company to send a sales kit to a relatively unknown tycoon in Buzzards' Glory. It was truly a different and better age.

The first problem was getting together the three cents for the stamp so I could take advantage of this opportunity. I managed then, as I do now, and soon my box of flower seeds arrived along with a picture of the cowboy suit for which I would work.

My paternal grandmother lived down the road about a half mile from me, and I immediately sized her up as a good prospect. A potato field and a strawberry patch separated our houses, and it seemed a long ways away. I had never been that far from home alone before, but my mother gave me permission to give it a try. I started on my journey. About halfway there I got tired and scared and sat down to rest and think things over. I could see that my grandparents' house was much closer, and when I looked back at my house, it too appeared relatively close; this amazed me. It was as if the two homes had been pulled together. Perhaps half an obstacle now and half later is less intimidating than the whole.

I regained my breath and crossed a ditch that seemed like the Grand Canyon and soon arrived at my grandmother's home. She met me on the doorstep, and I looked back at my house that was now twice as far away as it was when I stopped to rest. I could not understand this, but I saw my mother watching me, and she waved to me with her broom and I felt safe.

My grandmother, of course, bought a packet of my seeds for a nickel. So did my other relatives, neighbors, one-legged Al Summers and poor old Aunt Lou (I wonder where she is buried), who ate the chicken that got run over, but not before she got our permission. Anyway, I finally got my receipts together and sent them off up north somewhere. My cowboy suit arrived several days later.

My next business venture was what you may call 'punch and pay'. Again, I got into this through the <u>Grit</u> magazine. If I sent my name and address to a company up north, I qualified to receive a card with about thirty-six perforated, numbered cardboard discs that, when punched out, revealed a certain amount of a few cents that the punchee had to pay the punchor, I being the punchor. Then when all these numbered holes were punched out, there was a grand punching of one larger disc to reveal the winner of a cuckoo clock. The next step in the scheme was to send in all the money and get two cuckoo clocks. One went to the lucky punchee and one to me, the persistent punchor.

These early ventures in business were demographically handicapped, as I have pointed out, but when we moved to the nearby hamlet of Belle Haven, many opportunities to make money presented themselves.

Soon after moving to our new home, I made the acquaintance of Johnny Johnson, a white male, one year my senior, whose uncle Jim Walkley was my next-door neighbor. Uncle Jim had a beautiful asparagus patch that amazed me because I could actually watch it grow. He also had a little hand-operated chopper which he used to prepare the asparagus for market. He had many edible end pieces and culls left over that he gave to his nephew and me.

We sold them for fifteen cents per bundle by going door to door. However, for two reasons that Johnny, being a year senior (which was a big gap in those days), carefully explained to me, I only got a nickel for each bunch. Since Jim Walkley, the donor, was the uncle and Johnny, the joint donee, was the nephew, and I, the other joint donee, was only a neighbor, Johnny had certain grandfathered or granduncled rights. Besides, a nickel was larger than a dime. Just to show his fairness, he said to me, "You take the nickel and I'll take the dime or else I'll take the dime and you take the nickel." (Johnny is now a wealthy lawyer and part-time judge.) Years later Cabell used this same logic when we had to divide up a duck and a goose. I then realized what had happened to me in the asparagus business.

My next sales venture was the purchase by mail of fireworks that I resold at a tremendous markup to other kids in the neighborhood. Johnny and I both participated in this enterprise. However, I readily had him beat in volume because I offered credit and he did not. My sales soared, and I can distinctly remember more than one of my customers saying on Sunday, Monday, Tuesday or whenever fate caused our paths to cross, "Where was you yesterday? I looked for you all day to pay you, but now I ain't got no money!"

I went busted and Johnny kept ordering larger, more powerful, and bigger quantities of fireworks.

Soon I was forced into manual labor. I began cutting grass in people's yards with a push lawn mower. I was told early on that the wealthy kids would make a living with their brains and the rest of us would have to use our hands. I was beginning to see that there was some truth to this.

BELLE HAVEN

*. . . I see starting from my little boyhood a succession of related occurrences
that finally when they all joined have caused this book to exist."*

Alex Haley

My move from the country to the little town of Belle
Haven did not mean that I was completely urbanized. After
a short walk or bicycle ride, I could again wander the woods,
fields and creek shores I loved.

I had not been in Belle Haven long when I was forced
to enter school. I never realized it at the time but thirty years
later some of my early schoolteachers, who were dental
patients of mine, told me that I was not an ideal student. To
be truthful, they all said that I was eccentric. In a way, I was
glad to hear that because I have been accused of inventing this
image to go along with being a sculptor, when, in fact, it was
always a part of my true character.

The first impression that dawns on my mind from this
time is the tin roof on the house we rented next to a real street
with a hard-surface road. I had my own room upstairs and
relish the memory of the noise of rain frustratingly pelting
onto the roof and not being able to get to me. In the back
yard was a huge pecan tree and, a little farther on, the
outhouse. At times, when I was making a run for it, it seemed

14

a lot farther away than it actually was. Near the outhouse was a hog pen, and near the hog pen was a chicken pen. There was also a small garden. I suppose this was a classic example (applicable to my father) that 'you can take the boy out of the country but you can't take the country out of the boy'. He always insisted on having a garden and a few chickens and a hog to butcher in the fall. My father's favorite thing was seeing things grow, and he told me on many occasions that farming was 'the prettiest work there was'. He said this with love in his heart, although the Depression had taken his land and forced him off the farm.

The hog pen was a little microcosm of adventure, danger, and intrigue. Volumes could be written about it alone. The highlights were the rats, chickens, and middlings. Middlings were a powdered or granular type of food, com-pounded from I know not what, mixed with water and fed to the pigs. I liked to help mix this powder and watch my father pour it into wooden feeding troughs. We could not always afford to slop the hogs with this specialized material and often supplemented it with table scraps. However, they were always fat for the fall slaughter.

The chickens also had slim pickings and would wander over into their swine neighbors' abode at times, hoping to pick up a few scraps. My first recollections of violence are the several occasions when I saw chickens caught and eaten by the sly and vicious hogs. Hogs like meat as well as vegeta-bles. Another bit of violence and excitement that I was exposed to at this young age concerned rats and hogs. At times, these vermin would try to sneak into the hog pen and grab a few scraps. My father did not like this, so he and I would sometimes wait behind the pecan tree with his .410 single barrel shotgun* and shoot rats as they tried to eat the food intended for the hogs. Now this was really a triumvirate:

*See "Cottontails — The First to the Last"

the three smartest animals on the North American continent, humans, pigs and rats (not necessarily in that order), all involved in that continuing eons-old conflict over food and subsistence.

Many homes in Belle Haven still hung on to some connection with farm life, as ours did. This is why I have told you about our particular scheme for survival. These were my first recollections of the town. As I grew older, my horizons broadened and I got to know more about the world beyond my own yard.

Belle Haven had a bank, doctor's office, post office, three country stores, a hardware store, ice cream parlor, movie theater, funeral home, dental office, two churches and a school. In other words, we were a fully-equipped small town with all the perks of metropolism.

The first institution in Belle Haven with which I became familiar was the combination grocery store and post office run by the Willises, Edward and Nannie V. They were two of the most genteel people I have ever known.

One day my mother gave me a quarter to go to the Willis' store and purchase a loaf of bread. A quarter was a rather large denomination in those days, and I was expected to bring back the bread and the change (approximately fifteen cents). The store was about two hundred yards up the street and on the other side of the intersection, and I was very proud of this important mission in a far-away place. I took the quarter and set out, determined to succeed. Soon I crossed the street and entered the store that adjoined the post office. The store included a meat showcase, wrapping twine, wrapping paper, and rows of food and merchandise. Naturally, I was a little nervous.

Standing at one end of the counter was the beautiful, and, I later learned, cultured and wonderful, Nannie V. I shyly expressed my desire for a whole loaf of bread and reached into my pocket for the family savings, the quarter, and after fumbling around awhile my thumb and index finger opposed each other, as primates' fingers first did a few hundred thousand years ago on the way to becoming human, and proudly produced the coin. Now, the consummation of the transaction and the successful culmination of this important financially-related mission was on the verge of being complete. However, as I reached the coin to Nannie V., it suddenly fell from my grasp onto the wooden floor, a floor black with use except for the silver colored and well-worn nail heads holding it in place. As I watched the precious coin roll around and around I anticipated no disaster. But suddenly it disappeared down a crack between the boards, and I felt myself instantly thrust into a horrible situation and began to cry.

In seconds, Nannie V. was around the counter comforting me and pushing a shiny new quarter into my hands. I was four and she was forty and I fell in love with her. Nothing has changed since. I never buy a loaf of bread without remembering that incident.

Mr. Willis was the postmaster. He was tall, slightly stooped, and he wore his silvery-grey hair combed straight back. He also wore a bow tie. Actually, I cannot recall ever seeing him without one. He was a little more distant and intimidating than his wife. It took me a long time to get to know him, but it was worth the wait.

The post office adjoined the grocery store, and he would run back and forth selling groceries and taking care of the mail. There were post office boxes for the affluent and a window where Mr. Willis would thumb through the mail to see if the appropriate name appeared on an envelope when someone didn't have a box. A heavy wire fence blocked off the rest of the room. Behind this divider between federal officialdom and the civilian public were a huge coal stove and two large bulldogs that would lie side by side near it, basking in its heat. I do not recall that the dogs ever moved, but I do not think they were stuffed. This little post office became very important to me in later years when I had gotten through the primer and had begun communicating with the outside world as a teenager.

There was also a bank, but I did very little business there; I invested all my money in shotgun shells, fish hooks and muskrat traps.

I visited the dental office only when my teeth were rotten and required pulling.

Dr. Burleigh Mears, the local doctor who had delivered me a few years before, once had to pick green grapes out of my nose and ears because of my early, unsuccessful experiments in human physiology.

There was not much for me to do evenings in Belle Haven at that early age except for a weekly visit to the movies. However, we did have a battery-powered radio we listened to. It was over this static-filled radio that I first heard about World War II from the radio announcer Gabriel Heater. I will never forget his words, which we were to hear frequently: "There's bad news tonight, folks." At that time it worried me, but I had no idea how it would affect me and millions of others much less fortunate. I was under the impression that the world ended in salt water to the east, west, and south and to the north with a vague demarcation called the Maryland Line.

Soon after this, my father heard about people working in the shade in the Newport News Shipyard, and he secured a position there at the unheard wage of $1.25 per hour as a pipe bender. He was always very proud of having worked on many battleships and aircraft carriers and carefully followed their participation in the war. Up until the day he died with the effects of asbestosis, he always kept all of the shipyard bulletins by his chair.

My father found an apartment for us not far from the shipyard, and I was amazed that there was not always one family per house in the rest of the world.

My father had moved our furnishings and decor in the faithful old family truck, after which he promptly sold it. Then my mother, father, sister and I caught the local train and headed south to the Chesapeake Bay Ferry Terminal in Cape Charles, near the mouth of this body of water which was to play such an important geographical and psychological role in my life.

I had never been on a train before, and it was a thrill for a six-year old. There were many strange-looking people. Coupled with the smell of coal burning and feeling the surge of power from the steam engine, this all combined to make an indelible impression on me. There was a man in a white jacket and red hat who walked up and down the aisles selling candy and beverages. I convinced my parents to give me a nickel, and I purchased some milk in a cardboard box, the first that I ever remember seeing not in a bucket or glass container.

After we arrived at Cape Charles, the second leg of the journey began. This was the steamer ferry to Old Point Comfort, the dock on the other side of the Bay not far from Newport News. The ferry ride of about twenty-five miles across the mouth of the Bay was fascinating for me as a child (and as an adult). Three of these boats plied back and forth all day and most of the night. Each ferry held about one hundred cars and trucks below, with a restaurant and lounge on the middle deck. The top deck housed the crew and pilot house. The Bay was full of dolphins then. My parents held me up over the bow rail so I could look down at these amazing mammals, staying a few feet in front of the bow without any apparent movement and leading our ferry across the Bay. After arriving at Old Point Comfort, we took the bus to our new home in Newport News and another style of life, one that definitely did not suit me.

After a few pay checks, my father acquired an old Ford coupe. We used this for visits home which were not frequent enough for me. Because I did not like the city, I spent all of my summers and at times part of the school year living with various aunts and uncles in the country back on the Eastern Shore. I enjoyed country living with those relatives but naturally missed my parents. So, for the first few years of my schooling, I frequently moved from country to city and back again. My Aunts Bernice, Dorothy, and Mary, and my Grandmother Custis all took turns caring for me, and each made a contribution to my upbringing.

The summers, of course, were especially fun. We pulled weeds, hoed, picked strawberries, gathered eggs and slopped the hogs. Each Friday night, after a bath and if the car would respond to cranking, I went to the movies with my cousins Melvin and Vernon while my aunt and uncle shopped. Saturdays and Sundays usually consisted of fried chicken dinners at midday, watermelon and a softball game. We did not have many store-bought toys but made stilts, slingshots, bows and arrows, and other things from whatever we could find.

After the war, my family moved back to Belle Haven to the same home. After four years, it was still vacant. This period is when I really got to know the town and its surrounding fields and woods.

I also became interested in the rest of the world, and the post office was my most important link with the outside. Through this portal passed my mail-order taxidermy lessons* and ten years later my degree from the University of Virginia. (I never cared much for ceremony, so I skipped graduation and had my genuine sheepskin mailed to Belle Haven where

*See "The Rockwell Connection"

20

it was handed to me by Mr. Willis instead of the governor.)

Another mail delivery I remember concerned a gun that I ordered. One summer, I saved all of my money to get a twelve-gauge shotgun from Montgomery Ward for $29.95. I purchased a money-order from Mr. Willis and sent it off. Thus began the long vigil for my gun to arrive. It seemed much longer that it was, I am sure. After the money had been sent off for a few days, I was in the post office every day when the mail came, watching as Mr. Willis took it out of the huge official gray mail sacks. Day after day I stood looking through the wire partition which separated the civilians from the federals, expecting that every time an arm reached into the sack it would bring forth my weapon, my ticket to independence and supremacy in the woods, fields and marshes that were not far away. Then one day a package, suspiciously looking as if it contained a shotgun, materialized from the mail bag.

I figured it was my gun and after the silver-haired, bow-tied Mr. Willis thumbed through the letters, I asked him if I had a package. I was let down when he said, "No."

Every day after school I repeated this procedure, and the long box with a Montgomery Ward label on it was still there. Finally I got up the nerve to ask Mr. Willis to check the package to see whether it was for me. Sure enough it was mine, and my arsenal, which previously contained nothing but a single-shot .410 gauge, was greatly enhanced.

There was a movie theater in town, and I received free admission for pulling the curtain. It was an old rundown building owned by Burleigh Mears, Jr., the son of the local physician, Dr. B. N. Mears. Later Burleigh and I became very close friends.

Occasionally, a live act would come to town. Tom Mix was there once, and Tex Ritter was a regular. He rode his white horse right down the aisle onto the rickety old stage where one could sometimes catch a glimpse of a scurrying rat. Since the show usually ran for two nights, Mr. Ritter (or Tex, as I called him) had some time on his hands, and he entertained a lot of us awe-struck boys by throwing bottles into the air and shooting them with his pistol.

We also had a shoe shop, where my shoes were resoled and re-resoled, and an ice cream parlor, where I purchased hunting and fishing magazines.

All the quaintness is now gone from Belle Haven. There is a new theater with an electric curtain and no more rats. Burleigh built the new theater next to the old one, subsequently torn down. Both were named The Idle Hour. The new one took several years to build and was Burleigh's dream of a lifetime but, as so often happens in life to those who don't have a crystal ball, a spoiler was lurking on the horizon. It was television. During the first few years of operation there were always big crowds at the movies, especially weekends. Everything seemed great. My mother worked at the soda fountain every night after cooking dinner for the family, in turn after working an eight-hour to ten-hour day at the local shirt factory.

As human habits insidiously changed, the crowds dropped off. It was almost imperceptible at first, then Burleigh had to book more expensive movies to lure a dwindling public. More and more people acquired the tube, sat home and watched it. Teenagers' habits also changed. Instead of holding hands in the movie hall and drinking cokes, they began to cruise the roads and shopping centers and drink beer or whatever came their way.

In the end, Burleigh's pride, The Idle Hour, home of Tex Ritter and Tom Mix, was sold. Soon afterwards, Burleigh died. Some say it was cancer, but I think there was more to it than that. He was a good friend and one of the most generous people I have ever known.

The bank, dental office, doctor's office, ice cream parlor, shoe shop, school, and both grocery stores are all gone. Belle Haven is now a sterile, uninteresting place, like a lot of other towns and villages on the Eastern Shore.

MILTON AND THE
THREE-STRING GUITAR

"Most historians agree that if music started anywhere, it started with the beating of a rhythm."

Aaron Copland

Milton Bailey had a very dark complexion and very, very curly black hair. So did his mother, his father Bill, and his brother Gum. Bill did little odd jobs around the neighborhood, and the mother took in washing. Everything seemed fine to me, but one day there was a tragedy in the family. Bill Bailey killed his wife and then himself with a shotgun. I suppose he got tired of a day-to-day, hand-to-mouth existence with no future and decided to end it all.

After this, I didn't see Milton again, and I have seen Gum only once. They both went to stay with relatives a few miles away but in another world by the standards of the day. Eventually, Gum went north and did well. Milton went south and disappeared into the bowels of Alabama. Today, no one around Belle Haven knows anything about him. Not many know anything about me either.

Milton and Gum were friends of mine and frequently stopped by to play or talk. They lived down the road, just out of town and across the road from the cemetery in an old run-down home. In this shack Mrs. Bailey had given me many a delicious lunch. Although I was too naive to realize it at the time, this probably stressed the family's meager budget. I now have a suspicion that when Milton insisted that he could eat only one chicken neck or one foot (not a leg which is a joint or so up) he was simply trying to be sure that I had enough to eat.

Milton was somewhat of a prophet. One day he and another friend, Hall Ames, and I were walking past our little Aryan schoolhouse. We had been out in the woods shooting our slingshots at a rancid old carcass of a cow someone had dragged into the woods and in which several 'possums had taken up residence. Suddenly Milton halted and pointed his finger at our school and in a manner reminiscent of Moses said, "Someday I'll go to school there."

He was almost right because he only missed his prediction by one generation. So it was that Milton's brain harbored thoughts about forthcoming changes in society while some of us were so confident in the status quo that anything different never crossed our minds.

Now you may not think that shooting rocks at a dead cow is great sport, but it is. After the poor old cow had been in the woods a few weeks, the black and white spotted hide, still relatively intact, was stretched drum tight over the ribs. In fact, every time a rock from a slingshot hit it, a resounding boom came forth. One would then see an opossum poke its head out of an orifice, either natural or unnatural. After putting up with this disturbance for awhile, the 'possums would finally leave their skin-tented cache and amble off to quieter places. It was great fun, and once we found nine 'possums living in the bovine. This cow had been an old friend. For years, we had passed her while going to and from school and she was the sole occupant of our softball field.

After the sport was over, we would hold our noses and retrieve all the rocks and pebbles we could find. Of course, someone from West Virginia or Colorado may wonder about this apparent false economy. But, on the Eastern Shore of Virginia, a rock was hard to come by. A good round, smooth pebble of the proper size for a slingshot was about as valuable a commodity as a marble or a steelie (ball bearing).

Now that you have been properly introduced to Milton, I will get on with the meat of the story.

I have never been musically inclined, have never been able to carry the slightest tune, and have had no sense of rhythm. (I did not know this at the time.) But one day my parents gave me an old guitar with three strings because I had been watching too many Gene Autry movies (one every Saturday night) and had become influenced by these films. Nowadays kids see movies that make them want things like AK-47's, knives, and drugs.

The guitar was supposed to have five strings, so I used a piece of my fishing twine to make it a four-stringer. Had I cut any more off the line it wouldn't have reached bottom at high tide. Thus, I was limited to a certain degree in my quest to learn to play.

I spent many hours practicing, especially on Sundays after watching Gene play his guitar the previous evening. I kept after it for awhile and did not seem to be making any progress. One day, I was sitting on the grass in front of our home, trying to create a tune, when Milton rolled up on his bicycle to chat about watermelons, bull minnows, ball games in the cow pastures, and other similarly important subjects.

As usual, he was wearing a pair of mismatched shoes, and they had no strings. But before we move on to the rest of his wardrobe, let me explain about the shoes. It seems that one of Milton's father's employers, and he had many, gave him two pairs of hand-me-down, worn-out shoes. One pair was Oxfords and the other was patent leather. Both Gum and Milton wanted the Oxfords, and there was no way around the problem. Old man Bill finally decided that each child should have one of each. This solved the problem in a somewhat negative way. There has been more than one Solomon.

A rope held up Milton's pants, and he wore his perpetual double-breasted, pinstripe coat with four button holes and four missing buttons and probably at least an equivalent number of owners. I thought of myself as a rich kid and, relatively speaking, I was. This always bothered me when I was socializing with some of my poorer friends such as Milton and Gum.

After the customary greetings and small talk, Milton became interested in my guitar. He asked me to play a tune for him, which, of course, I did. He did not seem impressed. He too had seen a few movies with singing cowboys. Finally, he admitted that he would like to strum the guitar a little since he had never seen a real one, much less touched one. Of course, I knew that it was hopeless, with all the practice I'd had without any results. But I thought I would give him the chance to embarrass himself since he was always a little uppity anyway. I handed him the instrument. He did a little tuning with the thumb screws on the handle part, and he had some difficulty with string number four, my fishing twine. Finally, he seemed to think he had things right, and he picked a little to get a feel for the individual melodic personality of this particularly fine instrument. Then, suddenly, for the first time, I heard real music from my guitar. Some of it was fragments of tunes that I could recognize and some was just a rhythm that he made up as he went along. I was embarrassed, my dog woke up and cocked his head to the port side and Milton was smiling and shuffling his feet to keep time to his tunes.

Many things went through my mind in the next few seconds. What was wrong with me? What was right with Milton? Would I be a failure at other challenges that I would face in life? Did my dog know that Milton was a better man than I?

I wondered if I should give my musical instrument to Milton, but I was sure my parents had made some personal sacrifice so I could have it. I also wondered if I would hurt them by giving it away. I considered all these things the same way that a computer figures so many variables, and I quickly came up with a decision.

I listened to Milton's tunes and watched him smile and sway. After a little while he stopped and reached the guitar back to me. However, I had already made my decision. I was never going to touch it again. Nor would I ever touch any other guitar. I told Milton it was his.

He put the guitar on his back, thanked me and left. I still can see him, riding down the cemetery road into the sunset, with the best gift he had ever received.

I know I did the right thing. Perhaps I should give someone my pen and notebook.

THE COME-HERE

"Take one arrow by itself and it is nothing, but if you take many of them together it is beyond your strength to break them."

Queen Phillipa of Portugal

We did not mind come-heres in our little village of Belle Haven, as long as they behaved properly. By behaving properly I mean a strict adherence to a certain code of ethics that meticulously evolved over a period of years under the guidance of my peers and me.

There was one come-here, however, who caused our little clique a lot of trouble. He was older than our group and a lot bigger and stronger, and he really made a nuisance of himself. We never knew where he came from or where he went. But fortunately for all concerned, he did not stay around long. Rumor had it that his father was a Republican and a Catholic. Many local people thought they were German spies, since these were the war years and someone had seen the father looking through binoculars out into the Chesapeake Bay.

The come-here stole bicycles, molested little girls, and beat up on members of our group whenever he caught us alone. Something had to be done. So we called an emergency meeting to choose a course of action. Right away, contrary to current practice, we ruled out diplomacy and unanimously voted for violence. Now, before you get upset about this, let me explain that we did not intend to use the kind of violence that drew blood or broke bones. We intended to employ the kind that only made the subject feel as though he would come to harm.

First we had to catch the come-here, and we knew it would take at least four or five of us to do this. To effect the capture, we first had to lure him away from town. One of his transgressions was stealing our rabbit traps. So I built a new trap and, on a day when he was killing butterflies in his front yard, I rode by in a conspicuous way to allow him to see me. As we had predetermined, he followed me to see where I was going to leave the new rabbit trap. I rode down through the woods, and when we figured he was out of screaming distance my cohorts jumped out of the bushes and overwhelmed him. We first tied him up and put a pine cone in his mouth to quiet him; then we proceeded to dig a hole. When this was big enough to hold most of his body, we paused and took a long time pretending to decide whether to bury him head first, feet first, or exactly how. We went through a parliamentary debate on each position because we were very fair and ethical people.

At last we decided that if we left his head exposed it would take him longer to die. That's what we did. We put him in the hole and covered him up with only his head exposed and left him to rot. In a few hours, just by luck, you understand, Old Nate, a local hermit whom we had presented with a rabbit and ten cents, came by. He approached, nonchalantly calling for his hound dog, which he pretended was lost, and just happened to stumble on the come-here. Of course, Old Nate wasn't going to dig him out automatic like. He removed the pine cone for negotiation purposes, and the come-here promised Nate the sum of twenty cents for digging him out. While Nate was digging, he gave the come-here a lecture about how lucky he was because he knew for certain that we had always buried offenders all the way in the past.

This psychiatric treatment worked for awhile. But eventually the come-here reverted to his old ways and actually seemed to hold a grudge against us.

So, we held another emergency meeting and decided on the need for another psychiatric treatment. This time we lured him out into the woods again by pretending that we were going to show him a treed raccoon. We had left my old hound tied to a tree, and he was howling to get loose, but we pretended that he was baying at the raccoon. While the come-here was looking into the treetops for the nonexistent animal, we all jumped on him and tied him up with the same rope we had used to tie my hound to the tree. We then forced him to go to our clubhouse (of course with another pine cone in his mouth), which was a little tar paper shack with an old, rusted-out wood stove for heat. We began deliberations in our usual democratic way, and everyone except the come-here had a say in his fate. We debated back and forth such things as live burying again, drowning, and pulling apart by Old Nate's big mule. The latter we figured out could be done either by tying the come-here's head to the tree and feet to the mule or his head to the mule and feet to the tree. It was with great satisfaction that we saw his eyes roll and his pupils dilate with fear as we discussed his fate. We believed that we were doing a lot to improve the come-here's personality, something that he could carry with him all his life. Of course, we did not allow him to get the faintest glimmer that he would survive this time, after being so lucky as to be dug up by Old Nate on the first try a couple of months earlier. He did not seem pleased when we finally decided that we were going to roast him alive. So we stoked up the old potbellied stove until it was a cherry red all over. It was so hot in our shack that some tar paper on the sides began to melt. The come-here was blindfolded, and we explained that it was in his best interest not to be able to see his bare bones after the flesh had cooked off, but he did not show any appreciation of our consideration. We decided that just as you pluck a duck before cooking it we should undress the come-here before cooking him. The first thing that we noticed was that Catholics were not in any way anatomically different from Protestants, and similarly, Republicans were not different in the raw from Democrats.

After denuding him, we were ready. We put a little more wood in the stove, then we all grabbed him, lifted him up and over the stove, and positioned him so that his rear end would be the first part roasted. We slowly began to let him down onto a big flat scrapple pan of ice water that had just been placed on the stove. The pine cone was removed so that we could hear him scream, and, as his buttocks went into the icy water and onto the ragged pieces of ice, he let out such a cry that we almost dropped him. Of course, the acrid aroma of the flesh side of a fresh 'possum skin thrown on the top of the red-hot stove was just a little of my own artistry thrown in. You see, we liked to do things right or not at all.

Suddenly our captive went from a boardlike stiffness to a consistency similar to that of a jellyfish. We were not sure if he had died or fainted, and we did not wait around to find out. We hastily untied him because we didn't want it to look suspicious if he were found dead in our headquarters. Then we ran back to town and tried to look as if nothing had happened. Later in the day, we were relieved to see the come-here back in his front yard killing butterflies. He seemed none the worse, except for a slightly disheveled look.

This time the cure lasted for about three months. Then one day he came upon a few of us shooting marbles behind the school and decided to steal some of them. Of course, this resulted in another emergency meeting.

We mustered our forces and kidnapped him again. This

time we realized that the ice-in-the-scrapple-pan-on-top-of-the-red-hot-stove routine was a hard act to follow. But we were determined to figure out a more impressive punishment and finally composed one. We took him out to the railroad tracks, blindfolded and with a pine cone shoved into his mouth. We had our usual parley designed for him to overhear. The debate centered on whether to tie him face down or face up, whether to have him straddling a rail or lying across it and various other refinements in the art of being killed by a train. Waiting for a freight train as opposed to a passenger train was the chosen method because he was so fat he might cause a derailment. Being a morally conscious group, we did not want too many innocent people hurt.

Finally, we made our decision and tied him on his back, belly up, between the two rails of the track. We knew a freight was due in a few minutes. Betting took place about whether the underside of the train would kill him instantly or just open his belly for a slow death. We could see the steam locomotive in the distance, and we removed the pine cone from his mouth so we could hear him scream, which was amusing in itself. He did scream a lot as the train approached, and we hid in the bushes watching this one-man show. As the train approached, its roar drowned out his shouts. Before the train had passed completely, we were back in town getting ready for bible school.

About this time, Old Nate, to whom we had given ten cents and a 'possum, came by hollering for his hound and was very surprised to find this fat white boy tied to the tracks. Nate was supposed to bargain with him for his untying but the come-here's nerves were in such bad shape that he was incoherent. Nate had to untie him quickly for free before another train came by.

What we did not tell the come-here (and I had forgotten to tell you until now) was that there were two sets of tracks, one northbound and one southbound. Being the kind of folks we were, we tied him to the track opposite the one the train was using.

It was not long before the come-here and his family moved away. Things were peaceful around town again, but I must admit that our little group missed him.

We never heard from him again. One rumor was that he was institutionalized. Another was that he went into politics. Either way he was a burden on society.

FARM LIFE

"The friendly cow all red and white, I love with all my heart:
She gives me cream with all her might, to eat with apple-tart."
                                        Robert Louis Stevenson

When I was growing up in the 1930's and 40's, farm life on the subsistence level in Virginia revolved around certain routines: daily, weekly, and seasonal. There was little planning or expectation, but this does not mean to imply any monotony, shortsightedness, or boredom. To the contrary, we lived exciting and wholesome lives. Unfortunately, that way of life is now extinct because of mechanization, especially the coming of the tractor and all of its accompanying equipment.

The tractor was so efficient, compared to the horse, that the farmer immediately found he could now tend much more land and produce much more food. Since the amount of land could not be appreciably increased, this meant fewer farmers were needed. Consequently, farms got bigger; they averaged sixty acres fifty years ago and average six hundred acres now. The efficiency of the tractor meant that the farmer needed fewer children and field hands. So the farmer had fewer children, and the children of the farm workers moved to the cities up north so they could find jobs when they became of age. In the 1930's, all of the farmers had three or four horses or mules. By the 1950's a plow horse was a rarity, and a farm with no horse is hardly a farm at all.

Along with these changes, the variety associated with subsistence farming became less common, and specialization became feasible. Today there are a few farmers who raise a lot of hogs, a few who raise a lot of chickens, a few who raise a lot of soybeans, and none who raise a little of everything needed for just plain living. In other words, they have taken a step away from the earth. Instead of raising many goods needed for living or bartering with a neighbor, farmers convert everything to money, and this is used for subsistence. Perhaps this is more efficient, but it has been my experience that when you do this, someone else gets a slice of the pie and the closer you remain to the earth the happier you are, and that is what it is all about.

As I have pointed out, city life just did not agree with me, and while my parents were working in the shipyard in Newport News as their contribution to the war effort, I spent all my summers and some entire school years living with my aunts and uncles on Virginia's rural Eastern Shore. They all treated me great, so it is difficult to say where I liked staying best. I suppose my Aunt Dorothy's and Uncle Melvin's was my favorite place because there I had a cousin my age. They treated me as an adopted son and gave me the same duties as my cousins. I thought of myself as a farm boy.

On a daily basis we fed and watered the chickens before and after school or before and after working in the fields, depending on the season. We also picked up the eggs, good old brown eggs, not today's anemic-looking white ones with pale yolks which are laid by hens deprived of worms and bugs. Also, there were the work horses to be cared for and the cow to be milked. Usually my uncle did this. I could never seem to get the hang of it.

I was always ready for a glass of fresh warm milk as

soon as it found its way into my aunt's kitchen. Most of it
she poured into broad, relatively shallow pans behind the
wood-burning cookstove. Here it would sit until the cream
came to the top. Then she skimmed off the cream to make
butter in her churn. After this, she put it into a press and
made cakes of butter with a decorative imprint on the top.
(This was my first contact with molds and casts, negatives and
positives.)

I suppose it is now safe for me to make a confession
since half of a century should be a sufficient statute of
limitations. When the cream rose to the top, I could not resist
an opportunity to put my mouth directly into the pan and suck
up the cream when no one was looking. This Spartan procedure left a little circular hiatus of white in the cream's
yellow surface. My Aunt Dorothy often noticed this, and once
I heard her say to herself, "I cannot understand the spots of
missing cream in my pans of milk." So now, my dear aunt
and second mother, you know the answer to the dairy mystery.

The farmer's year began with spring plowing. Of
course, being in school, we missed much of the activity but
did our share on evenings, Saturdays, and holidays. It took a
long time to plow forty or fifty acres with nothing but a horse
and a single plow. It was started when the weather allowed
in February and continued into April or May. Nowadays one
big tractor can do more in one day than we all did in a month.

The horses were very reluctant to go to the field in the
morning. It usually took a lot of coaxing to get them out
there. However, at the end of the day they were eager to
return home, knowing that rest, food, and water awaited. If
there were no rain in the forecast, we would unhitch the horse
at the end of the day, leave the plow and most of the harness
in the field, and mount up for a quick ride home. After the
plowing there was disking and dragging before planting, but
this went much faster.

One of the biggest jobs we had was pulling weeds and hoeing. No herbicides were ever used, and there were significantly fewer weeds than you have now. Somehow I think that the weeds have become immune to poison. Also, nowadays you don't have many children willing to pull weeds for room and board, and, of course, the families are also smaller. So it takes more poison to kill the weeds and grass, their immunity is keeping ahead of modern chemistry, and the art of pulling them by hand is lost.

This is not unlike penicillin, which was so devastating to germs and so effective when it was introduced. Later, however, the germ mutated and became resistant to this wonder drug because of its overuse, and, by now, the doctor had forgotten, or never learned, more simple remedies.

Nearly all of the small farms planted the same thing: white potatoes, sweet potatoes, tomatoes, corn, strawberries, and sometimes string beans. No one knew what soybeans were in those days. Crops were grown for the market and for home use, either eaten fresh or preserved for winter.

The main livestock, other than the utilitarian horse, consisted of pigs, chickens, and a cow. The livestock was for home consumption, except, of course, the surplus of eggs, which was traded for groceries. Everybody had a cow and a calf, and someone must have had a bull, but I never saw him. Very few ducks and geese were kept, and I think this was because of the plentiful supply of wild ones available from September through March. We were very close to the Chesapeake with all its tidal creeks and marshes, and waterfowl was there for the taking.

To me, and I believe everyone else on the farm, the harvest was more fun than the preparation of the land, the planting of the crop, or the nurturing of it. Though I must admit it is wonderful to see and pleasing to hear the laughing gulls follow the plow while your nose is full of the fresh-earth smell of spring.

Strawberries were the first things harvested. This began in May, and the children had a special feeling about it, probably for a variety of reasons. One was because by May we were all tired of school (I was tired of it in September), and picking strawberries was a genuine legitimate excuse to be absent. Obviously, the beauty and taste of the berry did not detract from its appeal.

What I really liked best was the independence the harvest afforded, along with the sort of free-enterprise feeling you had because the more you picked, the more you made. It was in a way a capitalistic type of work in which you had no boss, and the only rules were to stay in your own row and pick only the ripe berries.

There were a lot of weeds and manure between Monday morning and Friday afternoon, but the end of the week meant a trip into town, so the long hours of toil were worth it.

There was a certain routine that my cousin and I followed during these trips with his family. First, we visited the five-and-ten-cent store to look at all the worldly wares; then we stopped to drink a soda at the drug store; then we saw the movie, which was usually a Western preceded by a serial that left us breathless and the hero and heroine in dire peril until the following week. After the movie, we met with my aunt and uncle at the local grocery store with enough provisions and culture to last exactly one week.

It was a good, simple, healthy life, enjoyed by young and old. But it is as extinct as the passenger pigeon.

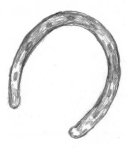

HOG KILLING

"That which dieth of itself, and blood, and swine's flesh, . . . and that which hath been sacrificed on the blocks of stone, is forbidden you . . ."

Muhammad

Nearly every farm family kept a few hogs, and, throughout the year, the children of the family took care of them. This was one of our regular chores, and we loved to slop the hogs. We fed them various foods, including table scraps, horse corn, and middlings. Occasionally the hog varied its diet by adding an unwary chicken to its meal. In those days, everything in the way of man and beast was an opportunist when it came to eating. The chickens hung around the hog pen in hopes of picking up a few scraps. As a result, they sometimes became the hogs' dinner. As humans, we ate both.

These hogs were like everything else on the farm from corn to cows, self-perpetuating. A sow produced a litter every year, some of which were sold at market and some eaten. Hogs were kept in the classical muddy pen. This pen was made with wood and wire as a fence and with some kind of shelter from the elements. The shelter was usually just several sheets of metal for a roof, with low sidewalls. One of our jobs was to keep adding fresh pine shatters (needles) to the pen. The pigs quickly kneaded these into the mud. At times, they were allowed to roam a pasture or glean the cornfields, but usually their world was limited to a small pen.

The culmination of all this care was hog-killing day after autumn's first frost. It was a joyous occasion (maybe not for the hogs); a holiday from school with all the farm hands, relatives and neighbors attending.

The day before the killing, all the equipage was readied. Knives were sharpened, holes were dug for the scalding barrels, and firewood was collected. Massive lard pots were brought out, the sausage stuffer made ready, and fresh clam shells were collected.

The killing began early in the morning because it would be a long day (short day for the hogs).

Some people just threw the hogs down and cut their throats. I am glad to say that all my folks shot the hog in the head first to stun it. This way there was not so much squealing.

Immediately after the hog was killed, its carcass was immersed in a wooden barrel filled with scalding water and half-buried in the ground on a slope. The animal was sloshed back and forth for awhile, then removed and thoroughly scraped with the clam shells to remove all the hair. Actually, this hair was the first product of the hog; it was saved to mix with plaster to give it strength and used for the walls of homes.

The next step was to hoist the hog up by means of a block and tackle held overhead with three poles. A short piece of wood sharpened at both ends was stuck through the Achilles tendons of the hog and a rope or chain attached to this. The hog was then hoisted into the air where it was eviscerated and allowed to cool out for awhile before being cut up. Meanwhile, all of the organs were turned over to the women to begin the scrapple, sausage, and lard process.

There was a definite traditional division of labor based on sex; no women butchered and no men made scrapple.

The small intestines were pulled over a funnel-shaped device, inverted and thoroughly scraped. While this was being done, the lungs, heart, kidneys, liver, and other edible organs were cooked in preparation for scrapple, which was the first thing off the disassembly line. I have never eaten anything better than this fresh hot scrapple with baked Hayman potatoes, and I have eaten in some of the best restaurants and diners up in Salisbury, Maryland, and down in Norfolk, Virginia. Some ingredients were common to both sausage and scrapple, except there was much more ground-up meat in the former, and it was left raw until the time came to eat it.

Hams and shoulders were prepared for smoking, seldom being eaten fresh. This was an art in itself. Everyone had a favorite recipe for smoking with variations such as what species of wood, how much salt and sugar and spices to put on the ham, how long to smoke, and so forth. Some of the best ham I have ever eaten was smoked with corn cobs. Every farm had a smokehouse, where the hams were also stored after smoking.

Cracklings were the first delicacy from a hog killing. These were by-products from the boiling of fat and skin to render out the lard. Big pots of cut-up fat were kept boiling all day outdoors over a wood fire. After the hot lard was dipped out and stored in lard tins, there was a crisp residue of skin and connective tissue left in the bottom of the vessel - the cracklings. These were very good and eaten on the spot by all.

Everyone who helped took home a share of the spoils, usually the items that were not to be preserved. A few days or weeks later, when the people who helped you killed their hogs, you were expected to come and help. In turn, you took home fresh pork. This was a much more sensible system than everybody killing on the same day, being short of help, and then oversupplied with fresh meat that was impossible to keep because of the lack of refrigeration.

On the days following the slaughter, there was a frenzy of preserving, usually by smoking and cooking and canning. Everyone is familiar with cured hams, shoulders, and bacon, but canned pork is now a thing of the past. It was actually jarred rather than canned, being put into airtight Mason glass jars before it could cool. There was a wonderfully secure feeling in winter when the pantry held a portfolio of canned pork on the shelves, along with the usual vegetable and fruit preserves.

As unjust as it seems, the family cow which spent her life bearing calves and providing milk, sometimes for more than one generation, was eventually eaten after she was unable to pay her room and board. The same thing happened to hens when they began to lie down on the job.

This, of course, was tough eating when provider-type livestock was allowed to reach old age before ending up on the table itself. However, horses and mules were not eaten, this was strictly taboo in our culture.

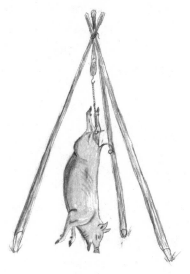

EASTERN SHORE CHIVALRY

"If you have any reason for not indulging a wish to speak to a fair woman, it is a bad plan to look long at her back."

George Eliot

Almost every native of the Eastern Shore is known for his chivalry. I say *almost* because there have been some slight exceptions.

What immediately comes to mind is the time my cousin, Lester Bull, got tossed out of a local restaurant/bar for some minor transgression. When the owner would not let him back in, he proceeded to gain re-entry with his chain saw through the unguarded northeast wall. Then there was another cousin, Alfred Simpson, on the opposite side of the family, who became annoyed when the bank unsuccessfully tried to repossess his Lincoln. The banker then obtained the assistance of a state trooper. Alfred's indignation caused him to take the trooper's gun. Another trooper suffered the same fate when he came to look for his colleague. However, being an extremely intelligent person, my cousin decided this was probably overkill and gave the lawmen back their guns and the banker the keys to the car. They did not realize that my cousin, who won a battlefield commission and a purple heart in the Korean war, was just playing around with them. Besides, on the next full moon there was a good run of peeler crabs, and he made up for the missing payment on his Lincoln.

Usually all was peace, quiet, and politeness in our little microcosm, especially when I was a child. I first began to note this chivalry at the county store, which I visited some evenings with my paternal grandfather.

There was always a group of farmers, fishermen, and other locals sitting around the store, playing cards or dominoes and drinking whiskey. You could say that this was their happy hour at their country club; it was pure country. Each person had his personal nail keg to sit on and his special position on the compass for his orientation to the table set up for the games. No newcomer was allowed to sit in that spot, and all the cardinal points were taken. The only way anyone new was admitted to this prestigious group was to fill a vacancy after someone's death. You could not just happen on this, it took a considerable apprenticeship. So there was always a group of younger men, usually in their middle age, hanging around the perimeter at a respectable distance, hoping someday to be accepted to the inner circle. Sometimes it was years before a space opened. If a man had not served a long and respected hanging-around-and-looking-on apprenticeship, he was not even considered for the opening.

There was usually a little drinking during the games, and I noticed early on a few basic rules of etiquette which went with the whiskey. Basically, a bottle or jug appeared and was passed around when ladies were not present (seldom were they in the store in the evening). Now some of these old farmers were rather grubby, and I would not have wanted to drink after them even if the container had been sterilized in an autoclave. There was always someone who chewed tobacco with a little juice trickling down his chin to be absorbed in his grungy beard. Still, the hallowed rules were followed. No one ever wiped the mouth of the jug after it was passed to him. It was permissible to wipe it yourself after taking a drink and before passing it along, but as things heated up this practice was abandoned. And, if the bottle belonged to you, you never under any circumstances looked at the level of the remaining liquid after it had made the three-hundred-sixty degrees.

One of the most prominent members of this group was Uncle Oscar Tilghman. He was a huge man with whiskers and a perpetual Panama hat. He was a model of chivalry, but some thought that he overdid it a little. You may gather from the following stories about him that I didn't get firsthand information. This is true, but the stories have become part of local folklore and therefore must be highly accurate.

Uncle Oscar occasionally went to church. One Sunday he sat directly behind a huge fat lady who had considerable cleavage in the stern as well as the bow. Uncle Oscar was one of those people who always liked to have everything just right. I can remember many occasions, when we'd be riding around his farm in his mule-drawn wagon, he would sight a lonely weed in his field of corn or potatoes and immediately send me off to pull it. Usually when I got back he would have located another on the horizon just a little farther on and off I would go again. It was this aspect of his nature that got him into trouble in church.

It all began when everyone, including the fat lady, got up to sing a hymn. Oscar never did pay much attention to hymns. His eyes began to wander and he noticed that the lady's buttocks had engulfed a great bit of her dress. It didn't show any signs of falling free. To Uncle Oscar, this was as disturbing and begging of relief as a tick on his coonhound's nose, barnacles on his boat, or a weed in his field. He just had to correct it. So, being a good Christian and willing to do unto others as he would have them do unto him, he proceeded to correct this conspicuous disfigurement and gave the dress a big tug. The fat lady turned with a scowl and muttered the unique and original words, "How dare you!" Well, this not only disturbed Oscar but also put him in a dilemma: he didn't know if he should replace the dress and hope the fat lady would forgive him or just leave it as it was. However, being the gentleman he was, he decided to replace it, although he knew it was aesthetically displeasing. So with his huge hand he began to poke it back into place. Of course, the fat lady did not realize that he was trying to correct a trespass as good Christians are supposed to do. She turned around and hit him with her purse full in his face but his beard absorbed most of the blow. Fortunately, this happened just as the congregation had finished singing and was sitting down and so did not attract much attention. The event, however, greatly affected Uncle Oscar. Afterwards, whenever he went to church he sat in the front row.

He also got into a bit of a problem at the annual county agricultural fair, again because of his genteel manners. It seems he had eaten a great deal of gypsy food and his stomach was churning about intensely. He was standing by the fence watching some horse races when he had to 'break wind', as he would say in Victorian vernacular. Remember, he was very mannerly. There was an unknown couple standing next to him. Oscar was involved with the horse race and had forgotten his manners, but the man took exception to the raw needs of nature and said to Oscar, "How dare you do that before my wife!" Oscar, being embarrassed and apologetic, right away wanted to redeem himself for any transgression, whether the uncontrolled natural type for which he didn't really feel responsible or the intentional, as with the fat lady. He knew that he needed to say something and simultaneously he was interested in the outcome of the horse race because he had a quarter riding on it. So he plunged ahead and replied that he didn't mean to 'go before' the lady and didn't realize that she had to go and the next time she could go before him. This was the second time in a month that he heard the words: "How dare you!" before receiving the crash of a purse to his face merely because he was trying to be polite.

UNCLE MELVIN

*"From one lofty branch the agile creature swung. . . through a dizzy arc to
a neighboring tree; then for a hundred yards maybe the sure feet threaded a
maze of interwoven limbs, balancing like a tightrope walker high above the
black depths of verdure beneath."*

Edgar Rice Burroughs

One of my favorite relatives was my Uncle Melvin
Drummond, probably because he was such a great sportsman
and lover of the outdoors. Actually, he was an uncle by
marriage, but I was closer to him than all of my blood uncles.
He was a man of medium height, with sparkling blue eyes and
a constant smile. He was quick in his speech for a Southerner
and was also very quick in his movements, whether he was
fox hunting, climbing a tree, or rushing a bunt from third base.
When shooting quail, he would frequently get three on the
covey rise and always two.

I have seen him unhitch his horse from the plow,
mount up, and ride to the call of fox hounds in the distance.
I never heard him cry out "Tally Ho" nor saw him don a red
jacket, but he was a gentleman in the truest sense of the word.
He enjoyed fox hunting as long as the roads were unpaved.
However, with time, we had paved roads forced upon us.
From then on, they were less suited to horses and more suited
to vehicles, and fox hunting became motorized and alcohol-
ized. Neither suited Uncle Melvin. He then became more

involved with raccoon hunting, but he did not shoot the raccoons out of the trees; he caught them alive, which he considered more sporting.

Essentials for this sport are a good pack of hounds, a nail keg sawed half in two, several potato sacks in good condition, a veritable acrobat to climb the trees (which was Uncle Melvin's forte) and someone to put the keg over the 'coon once it had been persuaded to jump to the ground.

Dignitaries, VIP's, CEO's, Governors, and other prominent people from Virginia, North Carolina, and Maryland considered it an honor to be able to go 'coon hunting with Uncle Melvin. His hounds, such as King and Tray, were to 'coon hunting what Secretariat and Man-of-War were to horse racing. Watching my uncle climb tall trees in the night and chase raccoons out on limbs fifty feet in the air, sometimes crossing from tree to tree, was a breathtaking sight.

I will not lie and say that he was better at climbing trees than Johnny Weissmuller. However, he was just as good. Besides, I have never seen Tarzan come down a tree in the middle of the night holding a live raccoon by the tail. After King, Tray and their cohorts had treed a raccoon, Uncle Melvin would climb the tree and try to convince the raccoon that it was safer on the ground with a pack of semi-starved hounds than to be in the tree with him. It was my job to put a nail keg over the animal after it hit the ground in an agitated frame of mind. We then safely got it into a potato sack, and the raccoon was ready for sale. And that is how I met Mitt Bundick, entrepreneur extraordinaire and middle man in the raccoon-relocation enterprise, who will be covered later in this book.

The animal was worth $2 alive and was used for restocking. There was big money to be made and it was a fun way to spend our evenings or on many occasions the whole night.

The chase of the fox, raccoon, rabbit and partridge was the primary recreation of the men in our rural setting, and Uncle Melvin always had an assortment of canines for each specialty. These hounds also doubled as pets and made great companions for the young, aspiring hunter.

Uncle Melvin was a very well-liked man and would take a lot of abuse until he was pushed over the brink. Then you had a problem.

Our local county fair, held near the village of Keller, was probably much like most others in rural America. There were horse races, hot dogs, pigs, cows, chickens, preserved foods of all kinds, sawdust, gypsies, merry-go-rounds and a variety of sights, sounds and smells. There were also, at times, boxing matches.

Once we were honored to have the U.S. Navy light-heavyweight champion come to our fair and fight any contender who was drunk enough, dumb enough or brave enough to get in the ring with him. Uncle Melvin fell into the last category. Goaded by some young farming colleagues, he put on the gloves. He followed the traditional role of shaking hands, then going to his corner and awaiting the bell. From this point on, Uncle Melvin got the rules confused. Being an overly friendly person, as I have previously stated, he was attempting to shake hands again after the bell rang when a vicious blow hit him right in his friendly, smiling face. Dazed, Uncle Melvin barely survived the first round, but he did not go down. Back in his corner, he began to come to his senses, began to realize the fight had started in earnest, and began to go over the brink. From then on, the Navy fighter found himself in very heavy seas until they halted the fight in the third round.

The light-heavyweight Navy champion was carried from the ring and made no further appearances as the fair continued through that week in August. He was not seen again, but they think he survived.

Uncle Melvin neither drank nor smoked and led a vigorous outdoor life. He was always ready to put down his own work to help someone else. He died of cancer at the age of fifty-six. Sometimes there appears to be no justice nor reason to life.

TALL TALES

"Of course you can exaggerate but you must stick to the truth."
                                                            Will Rogers

When I was a child, the Chesapeake Bay and all its inlets were full of clams. Not only were they plentiful, but they were easy to get. So I'm not sure why Uncle Melvin and his father, Ellis, decided to go clamming the hard way, but they did. Despite the general abundance of clams, even more could be found in inlet channels than in shallow water, so I suppose that is what enticed Uncle Melvin and his father to 'build a better mousetrap'.

My mother and I used to go clamming with Ellis in the normal, ordinary, run-of-the-mill way. We just went out to a shallow sand bar where the water was knee-high or so and anchored the boat. Then we got into the water and pushed the rake through the sand until there was contact with a clam buried just beneath the surface. Then the rake was reversed and the unsuspecting clam pulled up and deposited into a tub with a rope running from it to the clammer's waist. Sometimes we would pick up two, and on rare occasions three, on one back-raking motion. On one tide it was routine for a person to get three or four hundred and Ellis would do much better. My mother would do almost as well, but she was never ordinary at anything important such as clamming.

Anyway, to get back to the story, Ellis and Melvin decided that they wanted to rake clams in the channel of Occohannock Creek where the water was about ten to twelve feet deep. Uncle Melvin was rugged, as I have previously described, but Ellis was even more of a diamond in the rough, although he was already fifty or so when I first got to know him. I often wonder what his father and grandfather were like. Both Ellis and Melvin were great sports. One of them decided that if you were on stilts you could wade out into the channels and rake the hard-to-get-at clams, giving the easy-to-get-at ones a respite, therefore preserving the balance of nature. (This happened before my time, so I did not personally witness any of it; nevertheless, it is part of local mythology and knowing Ellis and Melvin I have no doubt this narrative is accurate.)

Their stilts were not the usual type which elevate you a couple of feet. They required a distance of eight feet or so from your foot to the bottom, somewhat like what you see the clowns using in the circus. Also, the men nailed a large flat piece of wood on the bottom of the stilts to keep from sinking into the mud. How anyone could navigate in the currents and waves on tall stilts and use a clam rake at the same time, I do not know, but Ellis and Melvin did it.

This adventurous team was actually based on Craddock Creek (the southern boundary of Melson's Marsh). But Craddock Creek was easy picking due to its relative shallowness, and soon all of the channel clams were captured. Then, one of the men (from my historical references I cannot precisely detect who was calling the shots, but at the time Melvin was a teenager so I suspect that it was his father) decided that Occohannock Creek would be more of a challenge because it was much deeper. In fact, it was so deep that a steamboat had a regular run into it to deliver and pick up passengers, seafood and produce for other parts of the Chesapeake Bay area.

These steamboats were quite large and always carried several hundred people plus a cargo of all kinds of supplies for the populace. They were our isolated area's main source of communication with the rest of Virginia. (Now there is a bridge-tunnel across the Bay and also a railroad and a highway.) These steamboats were an institutional lifeline to our community and something with which no one was supposed to tamper, not that Ellis and Melvin intentionally tampered with them. But they did ruin the safety record of one of them and hold up commerce and transportation for several tides because of their unconventional clamming methods.

It happened on a bright, hot August day in the late 1920's. The clammers, having tired of the shallow channels in Craddock Creek, decided to entertain themselves on this Sunday afternoon by trying the deeper channel of Occohannock Creek.

After church, the pair headed south along the shores of the Chesapeake in Ellis' one-cylinder clam boat and hung a port turn into the Occohannock, where they anchored, put on their stilts, and gradually worked their way into the channel. After really getting the hang of this deeper water, they began to rake in clams, clams that never had before been subjected to molestation and were no doubt secure in their thoughts that they were safe in these deep waters whose virgin bottom had never before felt the steel prongs of a rake.

At this time, the steamer made its weekly appearance at the mouth of the creek and began moving up the channel toward its dock at Morley's Wharf, farther up Occohannock Creek. I suppose the captain had seen clammers and crabbers walking with their real feet on the bottom of the bars and shores of many creeks and rivers. This was natural enough in those good old days before plastic cards, highways, automobiles, fax machines and television, when man lived much closer to nature.

As the confident-yet-cautious captain guided his ship up the channel on this sultry afternoon with mobs of overheated passengers eager to disembark, something a little strange appeared before him as he peered out of the pilot house. Here, dead ahead, were two men clamming with water up to their waists and walking right along raking up clams and putting them into washing tubs trailing by ropes to each of their waists.

The captain was puzzled, not by how these men were walking in the channel but how he, who had navigated this unchanging channel for decades, had gotten off course. It was immediately obvious to him that the water depth was the distance from the men's waist to their feet, no more, no less and about four feet. He immediately did the only thing there was to do, and that was to go hard to the port (or the starboard, I'm not absolutely sure on this point) to avoid running aground in the shallow water in which the clammers were walking. These bayside channels are frequently very narrow, and before the captain could think over the confusing situation the hull of the hulking two-hundred-foot steamer ran solidly aground on a sand bar.

In a situation like this, all is not lost if luck is with you and you have ample flood tide in your immediate future. However, in this instance, the tide was not only at its peak but, due to the full moon, was higher than normal.

If the boat could not be floated off the bar on the next high tide, it could be a month before another opportunity presented itself. There were supplies for the local stores aboard, produce waiting at the dock to go to Norfolk and Baltimore, many hot passengers eager to disembark and an equal number on shore ready to embark. Besides, the captain's spotless record was at stake.

I am not sure of the reaction of Melvin and his father, but I suppose they went back up the Bay and home to Craddock Creek.

The next day at high tide would, if nature stuck to her routine, be the only chance for a month to get the boat free. All the produce and passengers were off-loaded to the nearest shore in small boats that afternoon. The following morning every mule, horse, and ox in Scarborough's Neck was on hand along with about three or four miles of rope and chain. Everything was tied to a hawser on the grounded boat and hitched to about forty mules, sixty horses, twelve oxen, and one billy goat. It was a grand affair. The ladies sat in the shade drinking lemonade and herds of children of all colors played in the fields. As the tide neared its peak, the boat blew its fog horn and everything and everyone pulled in unison as the propellers churned in the mud. The boat did not move. A rest was called and as the tide rose it was monitored on a stick in the mud by a Captain Dize, a retired oysterman. Then he announced that the tide would be no higher, not only that day but possibly for a year, barring a storm. All living things in the area including women and children attached themselves to the hame lines (tack people will know what they are) and again the boat whistle blew and the propeller churned and the boat began to move, almost imperceptibly at first; then, suddenly it was off the bar.

Thus ended one of the most exciting, challenging, invigorating, and entertaining experiences to that date, some say to this day, in the lives of the people of Scarborough's Neck. I am proud to say I knew the two people responsible.

COTTONTAILS-
THE FIRST TO THE LAST

"All hale, red-blooded boys are savage, the best and boldest the savagest, fond of hunting and fishing. But when thoughtless childhood is past, the best rise the highest above all this bloody flesh and sport business. . ."

John Muir

This story began with a bumper butter bean crop in 1933. My father, uncle, and grandfather were struggling farmers during the Depression, as well as before and after. This particular year they had rented about thirty acres to supplement their plantings on the small farm they owned.

The acreage was called Battle Point because a battle was fought there during the Revolutionary War. It was a beautiful spot on the shores of the Chesapeake Bay between Nassawadox and Occohannock Creeks about a mile from our home in Buzzards' Glory.

For once, everything in the uncertain business of farming went right. I can only surmise that they planted the beans on the full moon because my father always told me that this was very important. They also got just the right amount of rain and, for some reason, beans were in demand. This crop was so beautiful that the landowner told his three tenants he would give them the thirty acres on the Chesapeake in trade for their bean crop. This was a temptation because my father loved the land (and I inherited this attribute from him).

58

Times had been tough, and there were bills accumulated at the grocery store and various other places, so they declined.

After the harvest, debts were paid off and a few new clothes were purchased for the family. My father decided to really splurge and ordered a shotgun and a box of shells from Sears Roebuck. His brother, my uncle Thomas, also ordered one.

These guns were relatively small .410 gauge and only took a two and one-half inch shell rather than the standard three-inch. They were made by Harrington and Richardson and would completely fold up; a feature that I found useful in some of my later poaching escapades.

As a child, I became interested in this shotgun. Once every two or three months, my father would allow me to shoot at a bucket or some other target with it. He used this gun to shoot rats in the hog pen but never did much hunting. Most of the hunters were on my mother's side of the family; all of the Custises were real sports of the chase. The Turners were more inclined to seafaring and craftsmanship.

One day, after much pleading, my father allowed me to go out alone with the gun into an adjoining field on what I called a rabbit hunt, my first. My father was a little apprehensive about my safety and not very concerned about the fate of any rabbit.

It had snowed a few days before, and some snow remained in the cornfield behind our house. This is where I intended to begin my hunt.

The .410 shotgun evidently had been neglected. The ejector would not work. The only way to get a shell out after you fired the gun was to insert a slender stick down the barrel and push out the used shell. In addition, the hammer would not stay back, so to fire the gun you had to hold back the hammer with your thumb and let go when you wanted to fire.

Armed and with a keen feeling of exhilaration, I began

my rabbit hunt, walking over little clumps of corn shocks and grass with patches of snow caught on them. One is not likely to bag many rabbits like this, and the proper way is to employ a pack of beagles to chase them. But even though I had no suitable dogs, I felt confident I'd find a rabbit. Indeed, the cornfield and snow made a picturesque scene, suitable for the hunting and fishing magazines.

It is hard to describe the feeling I had on this first hunt. Perhaps you have had similar feelings, not necessarily related to rabbits or hunting but to something new at a stage in life when many things were new. Rabbits were not new. I had seen many, beginning with a nest of them in my mother's strawberry patch. Guns were not new because my father had let me target practice often. Also, my uncles and grandfather, on the Custis side of the family, all had guns and hunting was a part of life. But this time was different. I was in control and could go to the hunt with the power of life or death over all the creatures I might encounter. It was a primeval experience that I am sure has some genetic explanation reaching back into the eons of time when it was essential for man to hunt for food. I started into the cornfield, my gun ready, expectations unlimited, and a whole world of sporting adventure ahead of me. I needed no partner and no pack of hounds, just my quarry and me.

Things could not possibly have gone better or quicker. I had hunted through the first small field and past some pear trees in which a few doves had been sitting until I approached. I entered the next cornfield, separated from the first by a dirt road; suddenly I heard a scuffing noise and turned to see a cottontail rabbit passing on my right side at a tremendous speed. I must have walked nearly on top of him while he hid, but as I passed he lost his nerve and decided to run, and in his panic he went in the wrong direction. As he ran by me with his white tail bouncing up and down, I raised the minuscule little shotgun, pulled back the hammer with my thumb, and then released it. Fortunately (for me, not the rabbit), the gun discharged. Either on his way up or his way down (I forget which) the rabbit fell over and out of sight in the grass, corn shucks and snow.

I immediately thought I would need to fire a second shot. I focused my attention on reloading and pushed a stick, actually the stalk of a dried weed which grew so straight we used them for arrows, into the barrel to eject the spent shell. Then I put in a new shell and was ready for more action. I was so excited that I had lost my orientation. The rabbit was not where I expected it to be. So I then began to look and look and look. After awhile I got so tired that I put my gun on the ground and continued to look walking in ever widening circles. Finally, and it was a long time, I spotted the unlucky cottontail. I was so excited I was almost afraid to pick it up. After some hesitation and indecision about exactly what part to grab, I managed to lift him. Then I went to look for my gun. In my excitement I had lost track of exactly where it was so I began the same procedure all over, walking back and forth and in circles frantically looking for my father's .410. After another period of frantic searching, at least equal to the first, I found the weapon. Naturally, I took both items back to my house, eager to show the rabbit to my father. He was understandably surprised. I think that he at first thought I had been scavenging the highway for road kills. I put the trophy into my bicycle basket and rode it around town to show all my friends.

This was my initiation into the world of hunting, an era which lasted about twenty-five years and brought me much pleasure and excitement. Occasionally, I hunted rabbits with hounds, but I never had the satisfaction to match that first outing.

The last time I went rabbit hunting, I was with one of my frequent companions, my cousin Melvin, who had an excellent pack of beagles. The hounds quickly found a cold rabbit track which rapidly became hotter. They jumped the rabbit and it took refuge in a briar patch. My companion was on one side and I was on the other and the hounds were squirming through the briars, baying. The poor rabbit had no chance and finally hopped out unknowingly, right in front of me. I put up my gun (one much bigger and more deadly than the little .410) and fired, hoping I would miss, rare for me in those days, but I did. My companion swore, the hounds bayed, and the rabbit ducked back into the briar patch only to be chased again by the hounds. In a little while, it reappeared and came running tippety-toe right toward me along the edge of the briars.

Again I fired, again the rabbit ducked back into the briar patch, again my companion cursed, the hounds bayed, and the chase started again. This time when the rabbit appeared and I missed the shot for the third time, I realized it was on purpose. My disgusted companion called his hounds and put them in his truck; I knew things had changed.

A few days ago, I went down to Battle Point where my forefathers once raised beans. It is now a housing development full of strange people and ordinary houses and small lots selling for $100,000 each.

The little shotgun with a notch in the stock is restored and will soon belong to my father's first great-grandson.

Changes are inevitable, in the environment and in the mind. Some are good and some bad, that is the way it always has been and always will be.

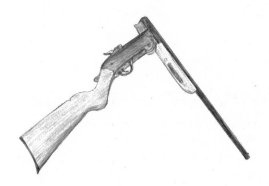

FIRST FISHING

"And now, I shall show you how to bait your hook. . .when you fish by hand at the ground. I will direct you in this as plainly as I can, that you may not mistake."

Isaak Walton

When I was about four or five and spending a summer with my maternal grandparents, I was introduced to fishing with hooks and a hand line by an incompetent and therefore unemployed field hand named Joe. It seems his heart was just not into farming. He was a couple of years older than I and claimed to be a fisherman in the class of Peter. One day he decided to show me everything he knew. In retrospect, he didn't know much. But at the time I considered him a giant in the art of fishing.

Earlier we had found an old discarded rowboat. After removing most of the barnacles and oysters growing on it and stuffing pieces of old potato sacks into the cracks to lessen the ebb and flow of the tide through its sides and bottom, it would float for awhile, if we did a lot of bailing.

We found some cotton twine and hooks and some old bolts for sinkers. Bait was readily available in the form of the blue crab. In those days one could net any amount of them around the shores. We put a few in a bucket and with a pole pushed offshore one hundred yards or so to a spot that my companion, in his infinite wisdom, assured me was promising. Then we sank the pole into the muddy bottom, about four or five feet down, and tied up to it.

One crab was selected to be sacrificed as bait and was carefully dissected with a brick and an old cultivator hoe. My partner showed me how to bait my hook and helped me put on a clean piece of meat with no shell or legs attached and informed me that this was the proper way. (Actually, it is not because a flawless piece of crab meat will not stay on the hook very long but will come loose as soon as a minnow nibbles on it.)

The twine was then unwound from the corn cob which stored it and the baited hook lowered to the bottom. We kept losing the bait, but finally I managed to hook a fish. This was the first time I had ever done this, and before I could get the fish into the boat I was also hooked. It was only a small fish, but to feel it pulling and jerking on the other end of a piece of twine held in my hands was a thrill I never fail to recall whenever I pick up a piece of string.

When the fish was at the surface, I lifted it aboard and watched in wonder as it flopped around on the bottom of the boat. Being a pig fish or hog fish, it lived up to its name and did a lot of grunting. I would guess that it only weighed about a half-pound, but it was very handsome with beautiful green and réd specks and the common panfish profile.

We stayed a little while longer, and my partner caught a couple of small perch. I was eager to show my catch to my grandmother so we soon pulled up the pole and went home. That evening she fried my catch on her wood-burning cook stove in a big black spider* and served it to me with fresh butter beans from her garden. This was, for some reason, one

*Frying pan

of the most delicious meals that I had ever eaten. It was very satisfying to be living so close to nature; no credit cards, frozen filets from South America, or microwaves.

Although I had a keen interest in fish in earlier times, I had never been fishing. Now, all I could think of was twine, hooks, and fish. My proficiency and experience soon began to grow as my father and other relatives began to take me fishing with them.

Back then, there was good fishing in all of the bayside creeks. These creeks are actually tidal inlets that pierce the small Eastern Shore peninsula every four or five miles of its north-south length. Their length and width vary, but two or three miles long and a half-mile wide is a close average. The peninsula-like piece of land left between the creeks is called a neck.

Fish do not enter these creeks so readily anymore, probably because of pollution from homes and farm chemicals, and one has to go out into the Bay itself for better fishing. Even then, it is not as good as it was just a few years ago.

One of my first serious fishing trips was with my elderly neighbor, Jim Walkley, and my father. In some ways, it was like the trip with my field-hand friend, except the boat didn't leak and we went farther offshore and had peeler crab bait (the blue crab just before it sheds its hard outer shell) and genuine lead sinkers made expressly for that purpose. The new white cotton twine was wound on a neat specially-whittled little board instead of a corn husk, and I had a new straw hat. In other words, one would have thought that we were outfitted by Abercrombie & Fitch.

On that sunny day in the summer of 1940, we left from Concord Wharf and paddled out into Occohannock Creek to the channel, dropped anchor and baited up with the back fin of a rank peeler. Soon the tide began to run, and we began to catch fish. We landed a variety, but what I remember most were the big croakers. I caught three on my own hand line. They fought the hook furiously. It was a thrill to feel the surge of power that in the beginning of the battle would pull the twine through my fingers enough to burn them. They were there for the taking, not as fast as we could throw our line over but at just enough of an interval to give us time to anticipate a little; anticipation is as important in fishing as it is in everything else worthwhile in life.

After we had all we could eat and some for the neighbors, we pulled anchor and rowed back to the old defunct farm-product dock. We loaded the fish, some still croaking (hence the name) and flopping, into the back of the car and headed home. We stopped at a local country store for refreshment that turned out to be a drink in a genuine glass bottle; it was not in a slot machine but a colorful cooler with a sliding top, filled with great chunks of ice and enough water to come just below each metal cap. It just seems that a soft drink in an aluminum can from a machine doesn't taste as good. Perhaps time has altered my taste buds.

I was an avid fisherman from then on. The first warmth of spring, when the shad bushes bloom, the wild asparagus sprouts, and the laughing gulls arrive, still makes me want to go fishing.

The first rod and reel I ever saw belonged to a neighbor who would lend it to me to practice casting in my yard. The rod was made of bamboo and had about as much action as a butter-bean pole. The reel was a heavy old Penn. This was a very awkward rig, I suppose, by today's standards. But I coveted this high-tech combination. One year, after mowing many yards with my push lawn mower, I finally acquired a secondhand rod and reel which I used for many seasons.

Even in those days I could see environmental changes which affected fishing, although I did not understand it at the time. It seemed that each year the good fishing got closer and closer to the mouth of the creek. Finally, one had to actually go into the Bay for a decent catch. It was no longer possible to just push away from the creek shore and shove a pole into the bottom and expect to catch fish. Nor could one walk around the creek shores and pick up as many bull tongue oysters as you could carry in a matter of minutes.

The early season, starting in April, was a favorite time to fish, simply because I hadn't fished since the previous fall. Fall was also one of my favorite times. It seemed that in autumn fish would enter the creeks in greater numbers than in the spring.

One of my favorite spots was Old Tom's Cove. It wasn't a true cove at all, and I never knew the identity of Tom. It was a small auxiliary channel close into shore separated from the main channel of Occohannock Creek by a sand bar about five hundred yards long and about one hundred yards offshore. The bar was always covered with a thick matting of eel grass and harbored countless crabs, small fish, and other marine life. The time to fish Old Tom's Cove was in the fall, and I especially enjoyed it in the evening when everything was still.

I never caught any really huge fish there, nor did I ever catch a whole lot of any one kind. What made this spot special was a combination of things: tranquility, closeness to the trees, being out of the mainstream, and, most importantly, the variety. Seldom did someone catch two consecutive fish of the same species. There were spot, croaker, mullet, pigfish, flounder, puppy drum (small channel bass), white perch, swelling toads, and an occasional speckled or grey trout (weakfish). There is nothing as exciting as the run of a weakfish in shallow water with not too much of a lead sinker to pull around.

As for my friend Joe, he really didn't have what it took

to make a good field hand. We lost touch for several years when he moved away. He later became one of the world's leading cardiovascular surgeons.

A few years ago we renewed our friendship and went fishing again. He picked me up at my studio and we drove to my dock. His white teeth were glowing through a sly smile as he undid the trunk lid to his big new Mercedes. In the trunk with a space-age cooler and graphite rods and seventeen-jewel reels were two corn cobs. Each was wrapped with cotton twine connected to two bright, shiny, new hooks and a rusty bolt for a sinker.

Joe still didn't know how to bait a hook properly; some people just never learn. And some never forget.

MITT BUNDICK — ENTREPRENEUR EXTRAORDINAIRE

"To me he's a diamond-in-the-rough type, a genius purely by instinct. He knows what the public wants and he delivers it."

Donald Trump

MITT CANTILEVERS A CAR

While my Uncle Melvin had only friends, Mitt Bundick had a mixture of both friends and foes, as it is with most of us. Mitt took advantage of every opportunity life presented. He made the most of every event, item or circumstance. He probably would have been a national leader or multimillionaire if he had a couple more years of education, which would have then totaled five.

Mitt was about sixty-five when I met him. He was small, wiry and extremely agile. He was only the second person I have heard of who could walk on water, or perhaps muddy water, or at least watery mud. I attempted to follow him through swamps and bogs several times when I was in prime physical condition, only to be left behind in a quagmire with a sack on my back filled with ducks, crabs, clams, or whatever was in vogue at the time.

To give you an example of his adaptability, when Mitt was a teenager, he shot off his index finger while trying to clean mud from his gun barrel. Soon after it healed, he discovered that the one remaining joint was perfect for loading his pipe with tobacco. From then on, he sincerely recommended that all serious pipe smokers have a joint or two removed for this purpose.

Mitt was as quick-witted and resourceful as any person I have ever known. Sometimes this was merely convenience, and sometimes it was an absolute necessity to survival.

One evening I stopped by Mitt's home to deliver a raccoon I had caught on a weekend home from college and I was just in time to see a good example of applied physics (I was taking physics in college). As I drove up, I saw a huge automobile (one of those twelve-cylinder models) in the deep ditch in front of Mitt's house, with a huge man climbing up the muddy bank. Mitt was coming out of his house with his pipe in his mouth, obviously enjoying the excitement. To me it looked as though the visitor would at least need a large tow truck to get out. I could tell at a glance, drawing on my college physics, that it would be impossible for the three of us to get the automobile above ground level again. In a way I was right. However, Mitt could do it alone.

And that is what all 125 pounds of him did. Without any hesitation or slide rule, or calculation or any apparent plan or forethought, he asked us to step aside. Soon, with a complex series of levers, fulcrums, props, and cantilevers made from bricks, pump pipe, chunks of wood, and worn-out hame lines, the automobile was, in a series of deft movements, soon out of the ditch and motoring on.

After this practical demonstration of physics, I could see that an applied knowledge of this subject was useful and I hoped that, when and if I passed my course, I would at least be able to get a six-cylinder out of a shallow trench with my 190 pounds and some specialized equipment, just like Mitt.

In all fairness to the integrity of this publication, and while we are discussing physics, I must also tell you that Mitt insisted that if he gave his shotgun a little push at the exact instant he fired it, he could bring down a duck or goose from a longer range than usual. Also, he insisted that a rifle bullet would have to travel a short distance after it left the barrel 'to get up speed'.

As accomplished as Mitt was at physics, this was not his forte. He was at his best when it came to what I like to call the power of positive thinking.

MITT AND THE BEAR DOG

Mitt had an uncanny ability to instantly recognize the monetary potential of any situation or object (either animate or inanimate). But I'm sure he didn't categorize them beyond being profitable or nonprofitable.

One day, while he was sitting in the barber's chair, a strange dog walked by. His instinct immediately told him to capitalize on this event. He jumped from the chair with the drape still on him and caught the dog, a large shaggy brute showing severe signs of mange. After a successful treatment of used motor oil and sulfur the mange was cured and Mitt decided to sell the canine creature as a 'bear dog'. He con-artfully worded an ad for its sale in an outdoor magazine and it wasn't long before he received a fifty-dollar check from a hunt club in Arizona. After waiting for the check to clear (there are people requiring scrutiny, according to Mitt), he took some boards off his hog pen, some wire off his chicken pen, crated the bear hound up and shipped him F.O.B. to Arizona. For weeks after that he was reluctant to answer his phone and scrutinized every out-of-state license plate with suspicion.

Finally one day, when he had regained some feeling of safety, he was opening his mail in the post office and came across a letter from Arizona. He handled the letter as if it were a cottonmouth moccasin, and, with some curses and utterances about people wanting their money back for a hound that had been completely cured of mange, he got up his courage and opened the letter; then a devilish smile came upon his face. The letter read:

Dear Mr. Bundick:

The bear dog that you sold us is the best we ever had. Enclosed is $50. Please send us another just like him as soon as possible.

Sincerely,
Mountain Hunt Club
Turkey Flat, Arizona

He shoved the envelope into his coat pocket and said, "Bill, let's go dog hunting."

MITT AND THE FROZEN LOCK

As an example of Mitt's resourcefulness when it was an absolute necessity, I recall the time we almost froze to death (or so I thought then) on one of Virginia's vast seaside marshes.

We had decided to go duck hunting one morning despite (maybe because of) a blizzard that was sweeping in from the northeast. We left Mitt's home in the blackness of early morning. This, combined with the snow, caused us, from time to time, to lose the trail across the marsh. However, after a long hike during which the snow turned to freezing rain, we finally reached the duck blind. But Mitt, being something of a poacher, had a padlock on his duck blind to keep other poachers out. The padlock was frozen solid, and the key would not even enter the keyhole, much less turn the tumbler. We were desperate, so it seemed, because of the fatigue and sub-zero temperature. However, while I was trying to decide if I preferred to be frozen in a prone or sitting position, Mitt came up with a solution. From the corner of my eye, I noticed a lot of steam rising as I huddled up on the lee side of the blind. I stood up just in time to see Mitt urinating on the padlock. After this treatment, he quickly inserted the key before the lock could refreeze and gave it a turn and we were soon safely inside.

He lit his pipe and took a drink of whiskey from his bottle, swished it around his mouth, swallowed and was ready to shoot ducks.

MITT AND THE TAME RACCOON

Mitt was one of the best marketers I have ever known. (I'm not bad, but am not in his league.) However, he was scrupulously honest and would go to great lengths to be sure that people got (at least part of) what they bargained for. He would buy and sell anything on which he could turn a profit. This included antiques, junk, dogs, cats, muskrats, wild ducks, whatever.

To keep costs down, he preferred to get his merchandise for nothing. This theory worked better with wild birds and animals than anything else. It did not work so well on his antiques and other inanimate objects, although he frequently turned a one-thousand per cent profit on these. Once I purchased an old lantern from him for five dollars. When the deal was consummated, he laughed and lit up his pipe. Then he received great pleasure in telling me that he had only paid fifty cents for it. Still, I was satisfied with the arrangement. Later, when I scrubbed off all of the dirt and pigeon droppings, I was elated to discover that it was brass and not tin, as we both had suspected. I did not mention this to Mitt but, meanwhile, one of his daughters had missed the lantern and apprised Mitt of its true value, which greatly exceeded $5. For a long time, he frequently implored me to return it for a complete refund and rectify this honest error on his part. I had the brass lantern polished like gold and derived great satisfaction from its bright glow which reminded me that, at least once, I had bettered Mitt. Whenever he visited me I made a point of having this beautiful lantern in a conspicuous place so I could watch him as he eyed it. It was not the money but the fact that someone had beat him on a deal that bothered him.

Mitt was good at the antique business and seldom made such an error, and when it came to live animal sales, I don't think he ever made a mistake.

One afternoon, I stopped by his house to discuss the market for fatbacks (small mullet). Mitt was in his backyard wrestling with a raccoon almost as large as he was. The poor animal had a definite disheveled look and was missing some hair that was scattered about in clumps. Mitt was in an even greater disarray, his long grey hair hanging over his steel grey eyes and his pipe in the right side of his mouth as opposed to the normal opposite side, a sure sign of stress. Freshly bleeding scratches covered his arms, and his shirt was torn. In his hand he had a rope with a worn-out collar attached to it. He was desperately trying to gain control of the raccoon. After helping him subdue the animal and attach the collar and place the 'coon in a crate, I asked Mitt what he was going to do with this unfortunate creature. He seriously explained that he had that very morning caught the huge raccoon in one of his box traps and with the Lord looking after him, he had that same morning received an answer to an ad he had placed in Full Cry* for the sale of tame raccoons. When I stupidly questioned Mitt concerning the legality of this transaction, he

---

* A magazine dedicated to hounds and raccoons.

quickly gave me a plausible answer. It was obvious that this big boar raccoon easily weighed twenty pounds. Also, it was a truism that it was now adorned with a worn-out hound collar. This in turn certainly made the raccoon at least partially tame, let's say one-fourth for round figures. Therefore, it was easy to calculate that at least five pounds, the average weight of a smallish raccoon, was tame. What could be more fair than that? Besides, there was no charge for the fifteen pounds of wild raccoon or the collar that was thrown into the deal without any thought of compensation.

THE END JUSTIFIES THE MEANS

Mitt would take on all kinds of odd jobs. I think he did this because of the variety. Usually, the jobs were small because he did not like being in one spot for very long. He never went by building codes or standard practice. He just invented as he went along, improvising, substituting, and gleaning pieces of material that could be put to some use for which they were never intended. Mitt didn't care much for precision. Mostly he just estimated. I frequently helped him on some of his patch-up jobs and became well acquainted with his methods. I could fill a 'How-To' book with them if I described them all.

As an example, I recall one job in which he was under an old home fixing a rotten sill. I was outside, reaching him the tools and supplies as he called for them. I had given him four or five chunks of wood off the homeowner's wood pile, about thirty feet of barbed wire, a piece of pump pipe, and a few assorted bricks. I was trying to imagine what was going on. There was some scuffling, then some cursing, then a pause, and finally Mitt called out to me in a tone that clearly showed he was on to a solution, "Bill, reach me a two-by-four and make it three hammer handles and a brick long." I knew then that this poor old widow lady's problem was just about solved. In a few moments he was out from under the house and we were off to go fishing.

Mitt, of course, didn't charge the widow much because of her situation in life. But that philanthropic attitude did not apply to everyone, especially Catholics. Mitt really had nothing against them. He just thought they were all rich like the Pope. And in our little microcosm they all seemed rather prosperous. Now I know they are probably the poorest people in the world as far as the whole flock is concerned.

Anyway, Mitt finally got a chance to do business with them. For a long time there had been a leak in their temple and no one could find it. New shingles didn't help, neither did new flashing nor any state-of-the-art caulking in all of the suspected defective areas.

Of course, the Catholics, being so well to do, had been dealing with licensed contractors and would never consider a patch-up artist like Mitt. But the problem existed for a long time and, whenever the Lord made it rain, water poured right down into the middle of the chapel. One Monday, after a rainy Sunday, Mitt was in the barber shop when the priest came in to get his hair cut. He started complaining about the perpetual leak. Mitt listened intently, especially when the priest got to the part about how much money he had spent with no results. Well, Mitt could resist no longer and decided to offer his services. He told the priest outright that he could solve the problem, carefully refraining from getting into the mechanics of the actual repair job. Mitt spoke so confidently that the priest, probably remembering the part about the meek inheriting the earth, decided to give the little man the job. Mitt put his price at fifty dollars and didn't want payment until it had rained. The other part of the contract was that he would have no help and answer no questions, it would just be wet or dry and nothing else. Well, Mitt was given the chance to earn the fifty dollars, and he only took a few minutes in the attic of the church, no ladders, no banging, no new shingles, in fact not much of anything. Mitt summoned the priest over and told him he would be back after the first rain. Soon, the Lord obliged. It rained for eight days and eight nights and lo and behold there was not a drop of water in the chapel. The delighted priest called Mitt over and gave him the fifty dollars for *solving the problem.* He also gave his blessings despite Mitt's Baptist heritage, and a big glass of aged whiskey, something Mitt said he never got from his own minister although he regularly attended church twice a year, once between the hunting and fishing season and again between the fishing and hunting season.

There never was another problem with the leak in the chapel, although Mitt has been gone now about twenty years; that is until very recently. The old priest passed away also, and the young replacement, not as tough as his predecessor, needed a heating and air conditioning system. During installation, it was necessary to put some duct work in the attic. In so doing, an old rusty jumbo size washing tub with a little water in it was discovered by the contractor, a very successful local heating and plumbing man whose father was a friend of Mitt's. It was, of course, removed.

After that a leak began to plague the young priest. He naturally called the last man on the job, since it had not been leaking before his work. There was some frustration in the months following when various artisans again were called in to try their hand at stemming the flood, all without success. The young man who installed the new system suddenly, one day, recalled how his father had once told him about Mitt's ingenuity in fixing a leak in the Catholic church that nobody else could handle. Immediately he went over to the temple and found the old tub which he had removed sitting in the garage next to a big black Mercedes. It was full of empty wine bottles, and when they were removed you could plainly see the various levels of water rising and falling over the years, leaving a record of rains and subsequent evaporation and more rains. It was as if whoever had put the tub in the attic had known that the evaporation rate would exceed the accumulation of rainfall. A fellow would have to be very sly to do that rather than try to plug up an elusive hole.

Before judging Mitt too harshly, don't forget that he didn't say he would *fix the leak*; he said he would *solve the problem*. It cost the rich Catholics about one dollar per year for fifty years to not have rain water dripping on their heads.

THE SAGA OF SALLIE BELLE

"Why taint nuffin but a skull — somebody been lef him head up de tree, and de crows done gobble ebery bit ob de meat off."

Edgar Allan Poe

Mitt loved to pit himself against nature. That is what he was all about. You might say he was an 'extractor'. He liked to live close to mother nature and, although he abused her, I think he loved her. He relished the game, the chase and being outdoors. He and I preyed upon the oysters, clams, crabs, fish, birds and animals of the fields, marshes and waters of the Eastern Shore. Even though you may consider this is a pretty complete list, it is not all; even insects were fair game, especially the honeybee.

Gathering honey is a delicate game and quite interesting because it is so different from all our other forms of local recreation and/or livelihood. It was a sport that took some long-range planning and one with an element of danger directly from the prey.

It was in the summer, when the flowers were blooming, that one completed the planning stage for a raid on the bees' nest for honeycomb the next winter. The first step was to find some honeybees. Usually, Mitt liked to look for them in hollyhocks or hibiscus around the ditches and borders of fields. They were not hard to catch. One just closed a bloom over them while they were busy collecting nectar. The next stage was a little tedious, since it involved tying a very thin thread of white silk to a hind leg without getting stung or harming the bee. Then it was released and you did your best to trail it to the nest by following the white silk beacon. Occasionally, one could make it all the way to the nest with a single bee but usually you just detected the general direction. However, if one moved to another corner of the field and repeated the process, he could get another general heading from a different vantage point. If both bees were going to the same nest in a straight line, you had a couple of vectors. Estimating where these crossed gave the catcher a general idea where to find the honey.

Of course, bees are very irritable when someone sticks a grubby hand into their nest and grabs some of their hard-earned honeycomb. So you have to wait until a very cold day in the fall or winter before reaping your harvest. The cold numbs the insects and makes them much less dangerous.

Mitt was always telling me about his youth, and the slightest thing would set him going. Anyway, on a bitterly cold December day we were zeroing in on a bee's nest deep in the woods when he suddenly stopped and said, "Sallie Belle is close around here." He peered into the tall bare oak branches all around, stopped, then took the ever-present pipe out of his mouth and, using the chewed up stem as a pointer, he looked almost straight up. I didn't know what he was pointing at or who Sallie Belle was, but finally I saw an object on a high branch. The object did not look as if it should be there. He let me figure it out on my own, and I finally recognized the skull of what appeared to be a dog hanging from a limb by a piece of barbed wire looped through its eye sockets.

Then Mitt told me the sad story of Sallie Belle. She was his bird dog, and he claimed she was the best he or anyone else ever owned. Mitt loved bobwhite quail hunting, and in the old days they were easy to hunt. The field edges and ditch banks were left rough, not like present farming practices, which keep everything clipped by mechanized equipment like a golf course. The birds had cover and food along the edges of the fields and were easy to find. Now, unfortunately, much of the timber has been cut, which gives the birds good cover, but cut-over woods are equally bad for the dog and the hunter. The other change is the soybean crop, now popular with farmers. The quail can sit tight, almost inaccessible in thick cover, and in just a few minutes run out into a cut-over soybean field and fill its crop and run back to the bramble. Even if you are lucky enough to catch a covey in the open, it will always fly back into the cover, and you will not be able to shoot singles.

Mitt acquired Sallie Belle as a pup in trade for a bushel of nick clams*. He liked her frolicking energy and interest in anything with feathers. He also knew her mother was a good bird dog. Genetics are as important in dogs as they are in horses and women, Mitt always said.

Sallie Belle proved her ability to cover ground, find birds, and retrieve cripples and dead birds in her first year with Mitt. She was a fast learner and also a fast runner, perhaps a bit too fast. Mitt figured she would slow down as she matured, but she tracked farther and faster on every

*Small hard shell clams, the proper size for steaming.

outing. One of her better attributes, being very steady on a point, made it downright inconvenient when she would find a covey a half-mile or more away and patiently wait until Mitt located her and flushed the birds.

As Mitt said, everything works out in the long run. It happened suddenly one day when Sallie Belle was about a mile out in front of Mitt, who was, as usual, struggling to keep up. She decided to cross a gut* and investigate the cornfield on the other side. Mitt saw her enter the low marshy area, and he started for his Model T to go around to the other side and head her off. Suddenly he heard his dog howling. He knew something was wrong. He called her and she wouldn't come; finally he found his way to her. She was a pitiful sight, covered with mud and mired into it. At first he thought a snapping turtle had a hold on her (I have seen them weigh sixty pounds and bite a broomstick handle half in two.) But it turned out that she had been caught by the front leg in a vicious otter trap. It was difficult to get the trap open but finally her mangled leg was free. He toted her to his Model T and took her home. After cleaning the mud off he examined the wound; he dowsed it with turpentine and sulfur, and bandaged it as best he could. As the days went by, it became apparent that gangrene had set in and Sallie's life was in danger. In those days there was no veterinarian in the area, and everybody did their own animal doctoring.

Mitt realized that he must amputate the dog's leg at the wrist joint or lose her. He gave her some whiskey, and this made her drowsy enough for Mitt to operate. It was a delicate operation. Sallie Belle's leg was held on a block of wood by Mitt's friend, Coby Salisbury. A swift blow of the axe, a rubber lid from a canning jar for a tourniquet, a touch of a red-hot poker, and it was over.

It was only a few days before Sallie Belle was up and

*Small brackish stream draining into tidal salt water.

around. When the wound healed, she and Mitt went quail hunting again. That was the beginning of ten years of the best quail hunting Mitt ever had. Now Sallie Belle with three legs was hampered just enough so that she did not range too far afield.

Then one day she disappeared. Mitt never saw her alive again. But a couple of years later when he was 'coon hunting at night in a big woods about a mile from his house he stumbled upon a dog skeleton. This was not uncommon because in those days not many people buried anything except humans; everything from chickens to horses were just dragged out into the woods and left to the buzzards. However, Mitt sensed something different in this instance. He directed his flashlight down at the bones; a front leg was partly missing. Closer inspection revealed the clean cut of an axe and Mitt knew it was Sallie Belle. The next day he came back and wired her skull to an oak limb high in the air.

After Sallie Belle, Mitt had given up on quail hunting. This, coupled with hanging her skull in an oak tree was his way of eulogizing his favorite dog. Mitt reminded me again that everything always worked out for the best as he pushed tobacco into the bowl of his pipe with the perfectly fitting snub of his shot-off finger.

I took another look at the moss-covered skull fifty feet in the air. Then we were off to find the beehive.

BRING THEM BACK ALIVE[*]

"You can judge the progress of a nation by the way it treats its animals."
Mahatma Gandhi

All wildlife fascinated me. I felt compelled to get close to it, look at it, touch it, be with it. Not being of wealthy heritage, I was also always looking for ways to make money. Profiting from wildlife and nature was a good combination, especially when no harm was to come to the bird or animal. Therefore, I had an early and keen interest in catching alive any animal with any kind of value. The way to do this was with homemade box traps. (Almost everything except the family truck and the radio was homemade.)

Before I caught it, though, I had to have a market for it. This is where Mitt Bundick, live animal dealer, came into the picture. I had come to know Mitt through raccoon hunting with my Uncle Melvin, who sold his live-caught raccoons to Mitt for restocking. Mitt bought not only raccoons but also squirrels, muskrats, 'possums, or just about any sort of wild animal.

The first creatures I exploited were grey squirrels. Mitt paid one dollar each for them. I had about twenty box traps on my trap line and checked them every day after

[*]Frank Buck's autobiography — he traveled the world capturing wild animals for zoos. It is one of the first books I read.

85

school. The trap was a long narrow wooden box with wire screen at the back end and a sliding door at the front which would fall when the squirrel hit a trigger as it entered to eat the corn bait. These traps were not big; inside measurements were about eighteen inches long and four inches wide by six inches tall.

Corn was the best bait. A few grains were sprinkled in front of the trap and some on the floor. You did not put out very much because in theory you didn't want the squirrel to become satiated before he noticed the whole ear of corn in the back of the trap. Attempting to reach this enticement, he would be apt to hit the trigger, a stick suspended into the interior of the trap. Even if the squirrel managed to squeeze by the trigger going in, it would be sure to hit the device on the way out when it would certainly be trying to take the ear of corn with it.

I would sometimes catch three or four squirrels a day. It was exciting to visit these traps and, at a distance, strain to see whether the door was down or up. If a squirrel were inside, it would become scared when I approached and make frantic attempts to escape. To get the squirrel out, I would place a bag over the mouth of the trap then pull up the door and, with a stick inserted through the wire screen on the back, nudge it into the bag. Then I had it. I really believe that's where the expression 'in the bag' originated, and people all over the world have been copying Eastern Shore trappers for years and not giving us any credit at all. But that's life.

Occasionally, I would catch a flying squirrel, which Mitt also bought. These were especially beautiful little animals with big black nocturnal eyes and soft fawn and brown and grey colors and a curiously flat tail designed for gliding.

I also learned to trap muskrats this way. These traps were set in a different terrain, and sweet potato was the bait of choice. Muskrats were easy to trap around freshwater streams and ditches but not in the fresh and brackish marshes where they were most numerous. This is probably because of the huge food supply available in the marshes, where they dined on cattail roots which, by the way, are delicious. I have eaten them raw many times.

While on the subject of box traps, Mitt once caught some kind of strange animal that was black with white stripes or possibly white with black stripes; he said it was hard to tell which. He had never seen anything like this so he put it in the trunk of his old Chevrolet and jostled it home. By the time he reached his back yard he had begun to detect a strange odor. When he opened the trunk, he was literally inundated with it. He figured that all he had to do was take his Saturday-night bath a few days earlier and he would be back to normal. But it wasn't that easy. His wife, Blanche, had to wash him eight times with vinegar over the next several days before he was odorless enough to go to a neighbor's home and borrow the encyclopedia where he found, under 'S', a description of the animal he had caught.

Occasionally, I would catch bobwhite quail or a cottontail rabbit. But there was no market for them, so they were immediately freed.

After I got to know Mitt better, he would take me on the rounds to his raccoon traps. Actually, squirrels were only a sideline for him. The big money was in 'coons. We caught them in the same manner and with the same bait and type of traps as we used for squirrels. Of course, the traps were a little bigger, about two feet long and ten inches by ten inches on the inside. One problem with catching raccoons was that their dexterity allowed them to put their fingers under the door of the trap, lift it up and walk out. To prevent this, Mitt weighted down the doors heavily with blocks of wood, pipe, bricks or whatever he could find. This kept the raccoon from escaping but made the traps very heavy to carry through the woods. Also, the weight on the door made the trigger less sensitive. I decided to improve on the design. My idea was a lightweight door with a catch on it so that when it fell it could not be raised until it was released from the outside. Mitt liked this, and I helped him change all his doors. Soon this idea spread all over our area, but I have not reaped any royalties or rewards of any kind for this invention.

My traps were not only ingeniously designed; they were well made. Consequently, if the traps were not well concealed, I sometimes lost them to thieves.

One snowy day with the ground heavily covered I went to inspect my raccoon traps. I carried a new trap and a potato sack with me, along with corn for bait, string, a hatchet, and some other gear. I inspected one, set a squirrel free because the market was off at the time, reset it and went to the next. But this trap was missing. Because of the snow, it was easy to see the fresh tracks left by the thief.

I followed them until they went directly to the trunk of a parked car and then went off into the woods again. I knew that the owner would soon return, and I was determined to wait him out. After awhile, he appeared and I recognized him as a local resident but not a close acquaintance. We made small talk about the weather, and I asked for a ride out the woods road. He readily agreed and told me to put my bag and trap on the back seat. But I said they were awfully dirty and that I would just as soon put them in his trunk and not mess up the seat. I knew, of course, my missing trap was in the trunk. Naturally, I did not have a search warrant, and being respectful of the Fourth Amendment, I did not want it to appear that I was searching. So before he could say much, I quickly opened his trunk to load up and, of course, there was my trap. I acted surprised and shocked to be in the company of a low-down thief, which I was not, and pissed off, which I was. He became very nervous and apologetic, explaining that he was irresponsible because he was a drunk. He did have a lot of notoriety in this field. I actually began to feel sorry for the poor fellow so I let him go, just as I had done for the poor squirrel a little earlier. I had caught him and made my point so I didn't press the matter any farther and accepted the ride to my pickup truck and forgot about it.

That is, I forgot about it until a little later when I learned that he had killed himself by going through a stop sign and into the path of a tractor trailer after he had been drinking. He wasn't really drunk when I caught him, but I am glad I forgave him.

JOHNNY WILKINS:
THE BEST DAMNED TIRE
CHANGER IN THE COUNTY

"Wolf Larsen did not laugh, though his gray eyes lighted with a slight glint of amusement; and in that moment, having stepped forward quite close to him, I received my first impression of the man himself — of the man as apart from his body and from the torrent of blasphemy I had heard."

Jack London

Johnny Wilkins was one of my favorite outdoor companions. You may say that he was my off-season colleague. We didn't fish together nor hunt game in the regular season. Instead, we went after such things as crows and bullfrogs and foxes when there was nothing else to do.

He was a muscular, broad-chested man with well developed shoulders and arms, reflecting his adaptation to his chosen profession, which was changing tires. He was also a bouncer at our local beer hall until well in his seventies. Johnny always had a serious look on his face, and I never heard him speak softly nor laugh nor smile. Still, as I got to know him better, I could tell when he was amused. Despite his profession and physical appearance, he was fanatically neat and also spent considerable time caring for his roses.

Johnny was the kind of man who never forgot a lesson. He and I prowled the local woods and fields along the back roads in his old International pickup truck, often stopping to walk, hoping to find something we could shoot and eat. On one occasion, he pulled his truck into a woods road and took his shotgun from the custom-designed box I had made for him. We started walking, looking for nothing in particular. I was trailing Johnny when suddenly he screamed out and began to dance around hysterically. Johnny had stepped into some human feces, right in the middle of the road. Though he could swear with the best and change big truck tires all day, as his huge old shoulders verified, he was a fastidious man in certain ways. From that day on he always avoided woods roads. While I walked the roads and paths in ease, he scrambled through briars and over fallen logs to get where we were going. This horrid experience had left an indelible impression on him.

I have seen surgeons do a poor job and butcher up someone, and I have seen indigents dig a beautiful ditch, expertly and skillfully. The former may be classed as incompetent but become wealthy and the latter deemed expert and remain penniless. Johnny Wilkins was an expert at changing tires and cursing, and no man on the Eastern Shore of Virginia could compare with him in either category (not that there are many statistics in either of these departments).

My first vague recollection of him and three of his four brothers was when I was about four years old. Now closed, the Wilkins Brothers' Garage was an institution in its day. (Two of the brothers are dead.) Another business has vulgarly and sacrilegiously taken its place. My father used to take the family truck there to get it patched up. I remember going with him and watching Johnny change huge tractor and truck tires and patch tubes and replace them while brother Doc welded and Horace worked on engines. Bill managed the cash register.

I had probably been there before, but on one memorable visit several things seemed to happen all at once. My father's truck had broken down, and I was with him while waiting for it to be put in temporary working order. I suppose

I was a little tired of the waiting, so I sat down on a black box that seemed to be just the right height and watched Doc weld and Johnny change tires as I drank a Nehi strawberry soda. It was just like a side show at the local fair: sparks flying, exhaust fumes, cursing, and many people and vehicles coming and going.

After awhile, they decided that the truck would have to stay overnight and, as our chauffeur was off that day, one of the Wilkins' wives gave us a ride home in a convertible. It was my first outing in a convertible, and I remember the wind blowing the curly red hair of the lady at the wheel.

Soon after we arrived home, my buttocks began to itch and burn. My mother quickly discovered that the seat of my pants had been eaten away by acid from the battery on which I had been sitting. This was a major problem because it represented a loss of exactly fifty per cent of my wardrobe of pants. With the family truck down, the future was not bright on a replacement. but worse was to come. That night I woke up completely blind and sore from burns of the retina. I remained so all night. The next morning, I was taken to Dr. Burleigh Mears' office, where he put some salve in my eyes. I soon recovered except for pink irises, which gradually went away. Initially though, everything was blood red, and it was a horrible feeling. I was left with only 20/5 vision, the result of watching Doc weld.

With the truck and me both getting older, I came to know Johnny much better. When I was a young teenager and he was about sixty-five we began to hunt together. What we enjoyed most was bullfrogging, not with a gig but with a .22 rifle. I never did like the thought of sticking a sharp piece of metal into anything, although I did practice dentistry for awhile.

Now I know that a lot of you will voice a protest against inhumane treatment of our amphibian brothers, but there is little difference in shooting a pig between the eyes and eating its hams and shooting a bullfrog between the eyes and eating its legs, although, in other ways there is a vast difference. During February and March there was a lull in outdoor activity. The legal hunting seasons were over. Except for mackerel and shad on the ocean side, and catching striped bass on the Bayside, there was no fishing.

Thus, the first warmth of April caused a stir in the body and the soul which called you to the outdoors. A million frogs of several species and various sizes bellowing and chirping add a special meaning to a meal of frog legs. There could be no better way to begin the new season than going bullfrogging and listening to the frogs herald spring's arrival by calling to potential mates.

Johnny had an International pickup that was a company vehicle. (His brothers sold International trucks at the service station, and my father and I used to build wooden truck bodies for them.) Johnny was very neat and meticulous in everything except his language. One day he came to my father's carpentry shop to get me to build a box to fit into his truck to carry his guns and Coca-Colas. Everything had to be perfect. After I helped him, he gave me a pocket knife which I kept for forty years until I lost it recently, and that night he took me bullfrogging for the first time. As time passed, we became fast partners in this business each spring for many years.

The prime reason for bullfrogging in the spring, other than it was the first opportunity for outdoor sport after a dull winter, was the fact that the grass had not had an opportunity to grow in the ponds. With little grass, frogs were easy to see, and they were very vocal because of the urge to mate. Our flashlights would pick up eyes of all sizes in every direction.

A typical hunt would begin by loading a small boat,

drinks, lights, guns and other paraphernalia into Johnny's truck to start the rounds to various ponds we knew to be good frog habitat.

None were big; some were natural and some man-made. The natural ponds suited me better because of the unspoiled scenery; plus, there was always much more attendant life (snakes, inedible frogs, and plants) which interested me. The man-made ponds were usually for irrigation and the deep drop-off and steep banks did not encourage much nature, although at times we did find a good supply of big lone bullfrogs, if not much else. In later years, some old irrigation ponds mellowed and have now become in tune with nature.

We would usually reach the pond by sunset, always one of my favorite times of day. Until it got really dark, there was not much frog activity. The action would begin with a croak here and a peep there and gradually increase until around nine or ten o'clock there was a continuous melody of all kinds of frog sounds, along with the characteristic bellow of the bull frog.

Johnny and I used .22 caliber rifles and, with a flashlight held near the fore end, found two reflective eyes just above the water's surface and attempted to put a hollow point bullet into the frog's head. Solid points would not work; usually, the frog would just swim away after being pierced by the nonexpanding bullet. We frequently got fifty to seventy frogs a night. That's one hundred to one hundred forty hind legs. I once bagged fifty-two without a miss.

As soon as a frog was shot, you had to pick it up immediately, before it sank. Sometimes we had to reach down into water a couple of feet deep to retrieve the frog. Usually the frog's white underparts would catch the light, and we could get it without too much groping.

However, one night an incident occurred which would alter forever our methods of retrieval. I shot a frog and it sank out of sight. Johnny reached down into the murky water and, after a few seconds, exclaimed that he had it and it must be a big one. He lifted the frog by a leg, and when it was above the water, we saw what we thought was a four-foot cottonmouth moccasin* holding onto it. Johnny immediately dropped both. The snake let go and I grabbed the frog. Johnny wouldn't let me keep it. He was concerned that the snake venom in the frog may have some deleterious effect on us when we ate its legs.

After this, we always carried a small net to pick up any frogs we killed, and just as Johnny would never again walk down a woods road, he would never again submerge his hand in a pond.

Frog legs are delicious, especially when fresh. The back legs are all that are eaten. They are cut off at the hips, which remain joined together, and the skin is removed with a pair of pliers. We would usually fry up a few around midnight after a hunt. I remember the legs actually would kick in the frying pan and sometimes save the trouble of turning them over. You can't get much fresher than that.

It was great fun to be there in nature's primordial bowels with a myriad of sounds and smells, pushing the boat under limbs and through grass, listening and looking.

Johnny didn't care much for cold weather, and this is why we usually confined our outings together to such things as crows, bullfrogs, foxes and stray cats, which could be pursued after and before the regular hunting season.

Johnny and I hunted together for several years, until college messed up my way of life. With time, the Wilkins Brothers' institution terminated with the natural death of one brother and retirement of another. Johnny was run over by a

---

*Years after Johnny's death, I learned that there are no water moccasins on the Eastern Shore of Virginia. I wish Johnny had known that because he was always worried about them when we were bullfrogging.

truck one Saturday night when he was in his eighties. He led an active life until that last instant. Actually, being run over by a truck on a Saturday night in your own hometown with friends watching is not a bad way to go if your time has come.

CHILDHOOD WATERFOWLING

"Wildfowlers since earliest times have for ever bewailed the disappearance of the good old days. 'Fowling,' they say, 'is not what it was, and probably never will be again.'"

Sir Peter Scott

If I could go back in time and re-experience any facet of my outdoor life as a child or adult, I have no doubt what it would be. I would again stand on the banks of Occohannock Creek with one of my friends and listen to the old squaws. Their calls, wafting toward us on a northwest wind whistling over Pole's Bluff, were interpreted as a challenge to go and chase them. And that's what we did.

By *we* I am referring to myself and one of my childhood friends, Johnny Johnson, now a prominent local attorney who has assured me that the statute of limitations has passed on most of our escapades and I can begin to tell these stories. However, he did suggest that I leave out the part about the dynamite when . . . well, that is another story.

The old squaw is so named because of its call, which supposedly resembles sounds made by old Native American women. Come to think of it, the long-tailed drakes call as loudly as the hens, so this may mean something to modern machoists, feminists, sex discriminators, etc. Even though the bird is not very good to eat, the males are especially beautiful.

Basically they are white with black, brown and tan markings.
They have pink bills and blue feet. These birds are great
divers and can stay down for several minutes. This ability is
what led to the demise of a few of them, as I will explain.

Johnny had a beautiful little rowboat with salty lines,
but it was only about eight feet long, with a beam of about
three and one-half feet. The boat had open gunwales that
were perfect for stuffing with salt-water bushes for camouflage. We each had a 12-gauge shotgun and at times shells to
use. Actually, Johnny always had shells. My supply de-
pended on whether I had cut enough yards with my push lawn
mower, done enough odd jobs or caught enough muskrats.

So we went to sea in this rig to see if we could get
close enough to an old squaw to bag it. One of us rowed and
one of us had his gun ready to discharge. The shooter also

kept the boat bailed out. The distance to the little flocks narrowed then increased to a half-mile as the birds became alarmed and flew off to put some distance between themselves and the little floating island which came closer and closer.

We did more chasing and bailing than shooting. And we were lucky we never swamped. We found that the birds would always fly just as we got within range, some flying from the surface of the water and others almost flying out of the water as they returned from feeding on the bottom thirty to forty feet down to find their comrades fleeing. After much unsuccessful pursuit we devised a strategy that was effective. We cautiously approached the edge of their perimeter of tolerance. When we saw a desired specimen dive to the bottom, we rowed like a Roman trireme about to ram an enemy. When the prey came to the surface, we had closed the distance enough for a reasonable shot. Once in a great while we bagged one of these beautiful, if not tasty, birds and it was worth risking one's life. However, after being pursued day after day they became wary and difficult to approach.

As we became more experienced in waterfowling, the idea came to us to have the ducks come to us rather than us go to them. So we began to accumulate decoys of every size and description. In our rig of thirty-one or so, only six were alike; and we purchased these from Sears Roebuck after pooling the money we made from selling firecrackers and mowing lawns. Many others we found washed up on the Bay shore. Some were given to us and some made by us. We practiced putting our stools (a salty word for decoy) out in the yard to get the proper arrangement. We knew certain basics about how to group divers as opposed to dabblers and what the sex ratio should be. We were extra careful to put out an odd number of decoys because Capt. Cabell Mapp had told us that no respectable duck would stool to a rig with an even number of decoys.

I do not know what happened when a duck flew by looking for company, spotted an odd-numbered flock and decided to join it. Of course, after he joined up then another single could not join unless some even number of companions was with him, and then there would be an even number remaining when he left. In any case, we listened to everything the oldtimers told us, including how well certain ducks could smell a human. To be certain, I thoroughly cleansed myself before each outing.

After amassing such a varied and large assortment of decoys, we were faced with a logistical problem. Neither of us was old enough to drive, and our parents would not get out of bed at 4:00 a.m. to drive us the three miles to the landing where we kept our boat. After a lot of experimenting with decoy transport, we came upon the idea of cutting a long pole and tying the decoys by the necks to this. With one of us at each end we could move all thirty-one or thirty-three or twenty-nine at once.

So, when opening morning of our first season came, we were prepared with decoys; guns held together with bailing wire, Duco cement, and rubber bands; accumulated shotgun shells and a boat. We had everything ready to go, and after a breakfast of peanut butter and jelly sandwiches, we were off.

When I mentioned the distance as three miles to the dock, this was not by the hard-surface road but almost as the crow flies. This route took us directly through the local cemetery.

We were both pretty brave, as you will learn from later stories. That was in dealing with live people; it was a lot different dealing with the dead. But we knew that if we had respect and did not step over any graves we would probably be safe. With this thought in mind, we began to wind through the little paths and roads and around and between the tombstones, with one of us at each end of the long pine pole strung with decoys, twine, and anchors.

It was a large graveyard, and we were quite far into it when we suddenly heard voices. Although heavily armed, we became apprehensive. Decoys began to slap into each other and knock against tombstones in our eagerness to get this leg of the journey behind us. Then as we rounded a brushy corner we came upon a group of people sitting around on top of tombstones and smoking cigarettes. This was all we could take. We dropped our decoys and ran, salvaging our precious shotguns. Back at Johnny's house we waited for the sun to come up and tried to reason what was going on in the cemetery at this hour. We never did figure it out. When it got light, we did find our decoys (somewhat battered) but no recent exhumations.

On another try, a few days later, and by another route created by the Virginia Department of Highways, we tried again. This time we got all the thirty-three, thirty-one, or twenty-nine decoys to the boat without any problem. We had cut a bunch of bushes to camouflage the boat and, after placing these around the gunwales, we rowed and paddled and bailed out Occohannock Creek to a spot that we thought was promising. We put out the decoys and took turns bailing and watching for ducks. It was a still, calm morning and not really a good duck-hunting day if such a possibility existed in those adventurous days of our youth. Finally we heard the whistle of a duck's wings and then a splash. The light was very dim, but after awhile we saw a form swimming around our decoys. I assume it was counting them to be sure the total number was odd, but before it finished we both fired and we had bagged our first duck over decoys. We picked it up but we could not identify it, a medium-sized bird with a glossy black head and a chestnut ring around its neck. After a little more bailing and waiting and freezing we decided to call it a morning, and while arguing about whose shot arrived at the duck first we pulled anchor and returned home with our prize.

Immediately we got out Johnny's <u>Birds of America</u> and learned that this was a ring-necked duck which usually prefers fresh water, yet we were on an inlet to the Chesapeake. I saw a flock of them today, about thirteen or fifteen in an old irrigation pond, and I wondered if any were descended from the one we killed in 1950.

The big game of waterfowling was the Canada goose. Every young hunter in our part of the country dreamed of bagging one of these migratory waterfowl. I was no exception in my bloodthirsty youth.

I finally got my first honker while I was squirrel hunting. I'd had no luck with squirrels that day but had been listening to a huge flock of geese grazing and honking in a nearby rye field. However, this field was on posted property. Although tempted and not above trespassing, I did not risk going to the field and doing a little poaching. I don't know why, I must have been feeling poorly; my notes do not explain my aberrant behavior in this instance.

I was sitting under a big tree looking for squirrels when I could tell from the tempo of their calling that the geese had taken flight. A few seconds later, I knew they were coming my way. This was exciting, but I figured they would be too high for a shot. Besides, it was early in the fall and the oaks, maples, and gums had not yet dropped their leaves. The only opening through the heavy red, green, and yellow canopy was about five feet in diameter.

As the flock began to come over me, I saw at intervals, a goose in the small opening. I tried several times to get an aim on one, but each time they disappeared behind the leaves before I could fire. I noticed that they kept coming at regular intervals. After doing some calculating, and when I thought I had the appearance of the next goose timed accurately, I fired at the empty space, hoping that a goose would appear just as the shot arrived. I was thrilled and surprised to see a beautiful honker's long extended neck appear about one millisecond after I pulled the trigger.
The shot arrived at the middle of the opening at the same time as the goose, which fell through the trees. I had won my coveted prize.

THE FIRST NOR'WESTER

"Within a space of five minutes a wind of more than eighty miles an hour will blow in, capable of capsizing even the largest craft."

James Michener

After a season of improvised duck hunting, as I have described, Johnny Johnson, Hall Ames (a mutual friend of ours whose name will appear elsewhere, except in instances where it is better that he remain anonymous), and I decided it was time to build a proper blind for ducks. We copied the style from one Cabell Mapp and I had built* but made it bigger and farther out in the Chesapeake. We decided to put it on poles on a sand bar in about four feet of water. In winter, from a boat close to the shoreline, we had often looked out into the Bay and seen large flocks of black-looking ducks which turned out to be scoters. Later, as we became ardent bird watchers down the sight of a gun barrel, we found that there were three kinds: white-winged, surf, and American scoters, all locally called coots. Also, there were lots of enchanting old squaw which frequently came into the creeks. The scoter didn't do that.

This mother of all blinds would be a huge affair with a box about five feet by eight feet and about seven feet off the water on high tide. It would have a large area to house the

* See next chapter.

boat, with poles and bushes on each side of it. Our theory was that it would appear so large the ducks would think it was a harmless tugboat going up the Bay to Baltimore.

First, we needed about eight poles twenty feet long by eight inches in diameter. Of course we could have bought these, but we knew where they grew abundantly in some beautiful pine woods. Borrowing Johnny's grandfather's truck around midnight one Saturday in September, we set out to cut them. Now I am sure that you will think we were stealing them, but that is not so. Actually, we were doing the gentleman who owned them a favor. There were too many trees in the woods, and we knew the rest would grow better if we thinned them a bit. The only reason we did this at such an odd hour was that we didn't want this man to see us and be beholden to us. That is the kind of people we were.

We hauled these poles to Johnny's grandfather's house on the south shore of Occohannock Creek, where we were using his barnyard as a staging ground. We skinned the bark off and sharpened the ends to a wedge so we could work them into the sand. A point didn't work as well as a wedge because a rocking back and forth motion pushed the sand aside better.

When Johnny's grandfather saw us getting ready to tow them out into the Bay, he told us, "The first Nor'wester will take her down."

We didn't pay any attention to the old man and began work. It took several weekends and a few missed days from school and loads of used lumber, which we got from an old barn. Each time we left the dock with a load, Johnny's grandfather would say, "The first Nor'wester will take her down".

It was a laborious job to build a duck blind a mile offshore in the Chesapeake Bay. First, the poles had to be worked into the bottom, about eight of them, as I recall. Boards were then nailed from pole to pole. We built a platform across the front four poles to hold the box where we would sit waiting for ducks and as a place to cook.

When we got a few boards nailed on, the seagulls and cormorants took a liking to this convenient perch in the middle of the Bay. After filling their bellies with fish, they would come to our structure to rest, sun themselves, preen, and perform other functions, all generally coming under the heading of toiletry. Each time we came out with a load of lumber, the blind was whiter and whiter and smellier and smellier. The odor became so bad that we had to wash it down each trip before we could stand to work around it. It seemed that nature was against us. But this was just a harbinger of things to come.

After we finished the framework and put aromatic cedars on it, the birds did not have so many convenient perches. Due to these two factors, things got better. When the blind was finally finished, we were understandably proud of it. The height gave us a panoramic view of the Bay, and we eagerly awaited opening day. Now don't get the idea that we much cared when the season opened or closed. But being in the Bay made one leery of federal game wardens who had recently been issued a seaplane for law enforcement. So we bided our time by poaching on land where we knew we were less vulnerable and had running room, until the legal season arrived.

One evening, a few days before the season came in, the wind began to howl out of the northwest. It blew hard all night, the first time that season. The next morning (while, for some reason my notes don't mention, I was dressing to go to school for a change), the phone rang a long and a short. That was our personal ring and it was for me. I was crestfallen at the message I received. There was an old fish trapper on the other end and he was furious. A big building had washed up on shore and on the way it had collided with his fish trap, doing considerable damage and freeing his catch. He had seen my name carved in the door of the wreck and was calling to get me to help correct the situation, which I did to the best of my ability considering my frame of mind.

Of course, it was just a coincidence that Johnny's grandfather was right, but we decided to place another blind closer to shore and in the protection of a cove; this worked all right. We made it pretty elaborate for a duck blind, well insulated with cardboard held in place with nails driven through bottle caps, spy holes, shelves of beans and crackers and coffee, and a small stove. We cooked some great meals in this duck blind. It was the same blind Sluby Wallace and I were headed for when we were swamped.*

We managed to shoot some ducks, but the important thing was the vista. Everywhere you looked there were flocks of ducks of some kind. I learned to identify them when they were miles away, not by their markings (you remember I was left with 20/5 vision after being temporarily blinded by watching welding) but by how many, how low, how high, how big, how little, how fast, how slow, etc. This information is much more important in identifying birds at a distance than counting their feathers or putting salt on their tails. I took great pride in making such announcements as, "There is a big bunch of red-breasted mergansers coming this way!", when others could not even see them. After a long wait, there would appear in the vicinity, if not over our decoys, "a big bunch of red-breasted mergansers".

We enjoyed the blind for several seasons; shot a few ducks and saw many, the tail end of a bygone era. In January of 1953 ice covered the Chesapeake, and like a huge floating razor blade pushed by the incalculable force of wind and tide, nature again took our blind.

*See "Boatwreck on the Chesapeake"

A GOOD VIEW OF
THE CHESAPEAKE

"Ain't nothing quite as cold as a duck hunter," he said, "unless maybe it's a cold, hungry duck hunter. . ."

Robert Ruark

As I grew and developed, so did my appetite for waterfowl shooting. I began to hunt with some of the older men in the area, and one of them, Cabell Mapp (whom I have written about elsewhere), became a boon companion. Cabell went through different phases of hunting, each lasting eight or ten years. When he tired of one particular sport, he would change to something different. When I first started shooting with him, he was just giving up quail hunting and concentrating on waterfowl.

Cabell had a little money which he had inherited. He was also, at times, a ferry boat captain on the Chesapeake Bay so he bought the decoys and outboard motor and also always had plenty of ammunition. I had energy, dedication and boat-building experience. Pooling our resources and expertise, we went into the duck hunting business.

There were many approaches to this sport on the Eastern Shore of Virginia. One could walk the seaside marshes or build blinds on the streams and ponds, all mainly for puddlers such as mallards and black ducks. We could hunt the Bayside marshes in the same manner, but most of these areas were privately owned, not by us. What was available to anyone, however, was putting up a stake blind in the Bay or creeks to shoot diving ducks. Cabell and I chose this latter method.

The usual stake blind was simply a series of poles shoved into the mud to form a rectangle with one of the smaller sides left open. Boards were nailed to each side of these poles, and saltwater bushes or cedars were pushed down between the boards. Depending on the location, the water may be from two feet to eight feet deep. The boat was shoved into the rectangular structure through the open end. There were many disadvantages to a blind left in this primitive state. First, with the rise and fall of the tide you might be too high up and could be seen easily or too far down to shoot at ducks settling into the decoys. Also, the movement of the boat impaired accurate shooting, and it was hard to keep warm in rough water.

Cabell and I decided that we could improve on this arrangement. We put in longer poles and more poles and built a platform above the highest possible level of the boat and built an air-tight box on this about eight feet long by five feet wide and four feet high. There was a small door in the back of this box, so we could enter from the boat, and a removable lid in the top through which we could watch and shoot. The sides of this box were composed of several layers of cardboard held in place with nails driven through soda-bottle caps. There were peep holes in all three of the business sides and a carpet on the floor. This little room was heated with a Sterno camp stove, and there was a radio but no television. A shelf supported various canned food, coffee and shotgun shells. We had three cups, three plates, three spoons, three knives, and three forks. I honestly cannot recall the pattern of either, but the utensils may have been stainless from the local diner.

We would arrive at these accommodations each day about an hour before dawn. First, we would lay out our stools (duck and goose decoys). Cabell was very adamant about how to do this, and I would try to maneuver the boat to his exact requirements so each wooden duck was in the proper relationship to the opposite sex wooden duck and to other species. The very critical formation, whether it be a 'T' or a 'V', was carefully laid out after considering the effect of wind and tide. Also, of course, the total number had to be odd. Then after this long and tedious ceremony was complete (in five foot waves, twenty degree temperatures, thirty-five mile per hour northwest winds and pitch black darkness), we would dump out a hundred pounds of bait that would lure any duck in the Chesapeake to its death regardless of decoys, and we were ready to enter the blind. By this time our fingers were so cold it was almost impossible to unlock the door.

The first thing we did was to get the stove going and begin preparations for breakfast. We had brown eggs, bacon, toast, and coffee, and you can't possibly imagine how good this tasted with the fresh salt air howling outside and the smell of coffee mingled with the aroma of freshly-cut cedars.

Of course, the conditions were not always rough even though we had better shooting when it was so cold and blustery that only a fool or a duck hunter would be out in the elements. One glassy smooth morning before light, Cabell and I had our stove going and a spider full of bacon and eggs with a pot of coffee perking when we heard a boat coming out of the creek. When it is very calm, sound carries easily over the water, having nothing to damper and absorb it. Even though the motor was putt-putting along, one could hear every word that was said. There were two old watermen in the boat, and they were discussing where to look for clams frozen out on the sand bars. Then one said to the other, "George, I smell bacon and eggs, did you burp?" George replied negatively to the interrogative part and added, "I smell them... and coffee, too!" Then the boat motor stopped and they had a discussion as to the emanation of these smells, but our duck blind remained undetected, and they finally started up their motor and moved on.

On these very calm days the ducks didn't fly so well. But on a flood tide a pod of porpoises would often enter the creek. We were always glad to see them because as they went in, the ducks would jump up and fly out, and we would often get good shooting for a spell.

Cabell always insisted that the porpoises ate ducks, so for years he kept a decoy out in the channel with a big shark hook attached to it. Fortunately, he never had a bite.

Even on days when we bagged no ducks, which was seldom, the view was spectacular. There was constant activity of some kind out on the Chesapeake. Huge flocks of surf and white-winged scoters were always there a mile or so out. Old squaws sat offshore on calm days in great rafts, and they were nature's music.

Cabell had certain ideas about duck hunting (perhaps I should call them dogmas) which he believed in religiously, and there was no way to dissuade him from any of these theories. I have already mentioned his odd-and-even theory on decoys. Another was his belief that when duck hunting in the morning, you would never see a duck until you saw a gull. So we would sit in our blind on a full stomach, sipping hot coffee while looking for that lone gull winging by out of the semi-darkness.

I recall one occasion when a pair of golden-eyes came to our decoys before the first gull. This was so embarrassing to Cabell that I knew it would ruin our whole day unless I did something. So I told him that while he was fixing breakfast I had in actuality seen a bird come by and that, on thinking back, it was probably a gull. With this he felt better about himself. I felt pretty good too, and we had a good day after all.

In fact, we never really had a bad day, and I would now trade a year for one more day on the Chesapeake with Cabell, watching the old squaws, hearing their incessant calling while we were eating bacon and eggs with the northwest wind howling down unchecked from Baltimore, pushing the cold aroma of fresh red cedar bushes right down into the bottom of our lungs.

Sometimes I would take girls duck hunting. I was convinced that they thought this was a real masculine thing for me to do, but I never seemed to make an impression on them regardless of what I did. The blind was, as I have said, quite cozy, as long as the heat was on. On one occasion, I took a very sophisticated female friend of mine out on a cold, black windy morning. She was very cold when we finally got to the blind but began to thaw after the stove had been lit for awhile. I shot several ducks and did my best to show off my wing-shooting which, in fact, was pretty good in those days. (It was still a humbling experience to go quail shooting with Uncle Melvin.)

After awhile, the ducks quit flying and my mind began to wander. I thought that with this show of wingshooting I should be rewarded with a kiss. However, she didn't see it that way and said, "I don't kiss boys in the daylight." That seemed final, but in this case it came to my mind that I had the upper hand. She was blond with blue eyes and had very fair and sensitive skin, so I thought I would turn off the stove and see how much chill her aristocratic body could stand. It didn't take the blind long to cool off because the wind was about thirty miles per hour out of the northwest and the temperature was just above freezing. She began to complain and wanted to go home to her mommy. But I stood my ground and told her that as soon as she was ready to compromise her standards and kiss me in the daylight I would take her home. As the temperature fell, I could discern that things were going my way and finally she kissed me. I got up the decoys and took her home to her parents.

She is still a good friend, but for some reason she married a guy who was richer, taller, better natured, and more successful than I. The only thing I could match him on was his taste in girls.

BOAT WRECK ON
THE CHESAPEAKE

"Now would I give a thousand furlongs of sea for an acre of barren ground, long heath, brown furze, any thing."

William Shakespeare

A boat wreck on the Chesapeake is not necessarily a serious situation under certain conditions. I have wrecked several times on the Bay. Depending on the weather, location, time of year, and time of day, the experience varied from life-threatening to just inconvenient, inconvenient meaning warm weather and daylight so I could swim ashore. But one particular wreck would have been very dangerous if it had taken place a few yards north of where it did.

It all began while I was a student at the University of Virginia. I really did not spend much time in Charlottesville and took advantage of every opportunity to come home. In those days, it was at least an eight-hour journey one way because of the hour-and-a-half ferry ride across the mouth of the Chesapeake and the attendant waits. When I say "at least" I am considering my mode of transportation, which included my thumb, my old suitcase with a big 'UVa' sticker on it, and my innocent country appearance. But enough of that; I could write a book on hitchhiking to and from college.

I had always thought I was invincible, but it became

necessary for me to have my tonsils removed, and I decided to have it done at the University. This was quite an experience. I was strapped into a chair, local anesthetic administered, and the procedure begun. With my mouth propped open, a wire garrotte was lassoed around the tonsils, and, with a bit of pulling and cutting, both tonsils soon were lying on the table in front of me. Then I was sent to the hospital for recovery. The next day, I was in horrible shape and could not swallow or talk. A three-year-old shared my room. He had also been separated from his tonsils the previous day but ran around laughing and hollering and drinking a Coca-Cola with no more side effects than if his toenails had been clipped.

When the doctor made his rounds the day after surgery, I convinced him to let me go back to my dormitory to study. He gave me a medical excuse to be absent from class for a week. This took me to the beginning of Thanksgiving vacation. I was free then, if I lived, for two weeks. But I fooled the doctor. (Actually, I told an outright lie and at the University of Virginia, with its rigid honor system, one could be drummed out of school if caught.) Instead of convalescing in my room and studying, I headed directly home and arrived late at night. My mother registered horror at my physical condition, but my mental condition was great because of the anticipation of two weeks to tramp the fields and marshes and hunt ducks on the Chesapeake Bay, with no worries about classes or studying.

After reassuring my mother that I was all right, I roused my old friend and neighbor, Sluby Wallace, and we made plans to go duck hunting the next day. The weather was promising, already blowing about twenty-five miles per hour from the northwest, with both temperature and barometer dropping. Of course this meant that conditions would be even rougher at sunup.

At 4:00 the next morning, I awoke at the demand of

the alarm clock and attempted some liquid breakfast. Since I was not able to swallow, all I could do was place some juice in my mouth, tilt my head back and allow gravity to cause some nourishment to trickle down my throat. After this I walked down the street to my hunting companion's house.

Sluby was, as were most of my friends, much older than I. My first tangible recollection of him was his giving me some insurance advertisement cards with bird pictures on them before I could even read. At one time, he was a great athlete and, like so many of our locals, almost made the big time as a baseball player. He was thwarted by some trick of fate, however, and I'm sure you've heard that before. Alas, he was destined to be an insurance agent. Going from door to door with a big black book collecting weekly premiums from clients on 'funeral' insurance is one impression I have of him in my mind. He was an avid outdoorsman, though, and this is why we were friends.

Sluby was the kind who seemed susceptible to bad luck, and this day was not going to be much different except for a couple of reprieves coming up in the next few hours which were to make a lot of difference.

Things started going badly for Sluby from the very inception of this outing. He went to the back porch to put on his gunning coat, and, when he opened the porch door, there was a terrible odor. He remembered that his wife, Kate, had been complaining about it for a week.

We loaded our guns and decoys into his battered old Studebaker. (Sluby had a new 12-gauge pump gun and was looking forward to trying it out.) After leaving the main road, we had about a two-mile ride down a bumpy dirt road to our dock. The strange odor came along with us. Finally, Sluby stopped his car and, after a thorough search of everything, found a well-decomposed cottontail in his gunning coat. After scraping it out of the pocket where it had become almost a part of the lining, we continued. The Studebaker was very drafty as Sluby had mistakenly tried to collect twice on a weekly funeral insurance premium and his client threw a brick through his rear window as he departed; so the air began to clear. Also, several baying hounds, which had been pursuing us as if we were prey, began to drop out of the chase.

By the time we reached the dock, the wind had picked up and white caps were breaking in the little inlet where I kept my small open outboard skiff, built the previous summer. We knew that it would be 'rougher than a cob' out on the Bay and that at sunrise the ducks would be flying.

We had a load in my small boat and not too much freeboard; it was built that way for fatbacking. However, I still felt invincible although I had to have my tonsils out like other mortals. We started out the channel in complete darkness with Sluby trying to pick up the buoys and markers with a flashlight and me at the helm. We were bundled up with pockets full of lead shot, and we were wearing hip boots. If we went overboard, we would have about the same chance that we would have had with a concrete block tied to each foot, regardless of our swimming ability. Seas were breaking all around us, and the flashlight beam readily picked up the whitecaps while we were trying to locate the channel markers that would tell us where we could find our blind.

It happened very quickly. Suddenly, a wave broke over the side. We took in a lot of water. We both started bailing furiously, but in seconds another wave broke over us and we were swamped.

As we slowly settled to the bottom, the decoys I had carefully whittled from leftover blocks of white cedar from my boat building business began to float away. I was grateful that they were going to drift ashore with the strong northwest wind. Instinctively, I grabbed my cherished old Winchester automatic and held it high above my head hoping to postpone its immersion for a second or two. I had these thoughts of preserving my equipment even though I could see no way I would survive.

As the boat settled toward the bottom and water came steadily up on me, I swallowed a lot of salt water. The strangling, coughing, and drowning evidently loosened the stitches in my throat and blood began to come out of my mouth. Then when I only had six inches to eternity (and Sluby less than that) the boat suddenly stopped sinking. It had hit bottom where there was not supposed to be any. However, I did not regret my navigational error. We both edged toward what we thought was the shore because Sluby saw a dim light in the distance. With Sluby's luck, I feared that it was probably a passing tanker on its way to Baltimore. But, as we closed on the light, we saw the tree-lined shore surrounding it and realized we were treading/walking in the right direction. I forgot to tell you how cold it was, probably because temperature had not crossed our minds until we realized we were not going to drown. I was so cold that I almost wished it had already happened so I would not have to go through the freezing-to-death process.

After what seemed like an eternity, we scrambled up the bank. Stumbling through briars and over fallen trees with the northwest wind at our rear helping us along, we headed for that glow in the trees which meant warmth. After walking fifty yards or so, we reached it and saw that it was shining from the window of a tarpaper shack and we could smell wood smoke coming from the chimney. We walked up to the front and only door, hoping that whoever inhabited this abode would have mercy on us and let us cross the threshold and live. To one side of the door was nailed a fresh 'possum hide, and leaning against the building on the other side was a shovel and a hoe, probably tools of the trade of the as-yet-unknown occupant. A few steel traps, an old plow point and a potato sack with a hole in it hung on rusty nails driven into the side of the shack.

We knocked on the door and it opened a crack. A suspicious eye looked us over; after all, it was early in the morning for a social call. Sluby pleaded our case, though we obviously needed shelter badly. I suppose that we were the only two blue-looking men the occupant of the one-room shack had ever seen, at least at that hour of the day. Finally the door swung open and with a graceful swing of his huge and calloused hand the old black man who owned the shack and our destiny beckoned us inside where we could continue living.

Our benefactor was quite ancient and, in his prime, probably stood six-foot-six. He was stooped by time and a life spent in hard labor, making other people's lives easier. He was dressed in a suit of faded red long underwear. He helped us take off our frozen coats and invited us to stand by his heating system, an old pot-bellied wood stove. The stove was already hot, but, seeing our plight, he stoked it with fresh wood and soon it literally vibrated with energy as it devoured the big chunks of red oak.

On top of the stove was a kettle of something that smelled interesting. Soon a pot of coffee was perking. Outside the northwest wind shrieked and the shack shook with the incessant gusts. I could not help but think that we were going to miss some good duck shooting. But we were lucky that we survived first drowning and then freezing in the space of about fifteen minutes. We could shoot another day.

Sluby continued to mourn the loss of his new gun and moved closer and closer to the red-hot stove. As we smugly thought about how the Lord had spared us and how grateful we were for His generosity, Sluby suddenly burst into flames. He had been too close to the stove and his coat had ignited. As I rolled him on the floor to put it out, I wondered if the grease from his forgotten rabbit had something to do with it. Still, this was a trifling compared to what we had been through and, with hot coffee provided by our gracious (if somewhat anxious) host, we were soon fine.

We were offered some breakfast and learned that our host was Long John Sample. I was cold more than hungry but reasoned that I would thaw quicker if I put heat on the inside as well as the outside. Long John gave me a big bowl of stew and I began to eat it, in my impeded way, when my brain thawed enough to connect the 'possum skin on the outside of the shack with the delicacy inside my stomach. I washed it down with some coffee and tried to forget the 'possums running out of a dead cow that kept coming to my mind.*

I hated to leave this shack, which was one of the nicest places I have ever been, and as I write this I can assure you that I have been to some fancy places, but this was one of the nicest, if you know what I mean.

Daylight soon arrived, so we decided to take the path out to the main road and with some dodging of falling limbs, we made it. It was not long before we were completely saved when a lineman in a truck looking for downed power lines gave us a lift to the old Studebaker. We motored on back to Sluby's house and went in to let his wife know that we were home safe, which didn't really impress her a lot.

Thwarted in our plans to go duck hunting, we decided to go after rabbits. Sluby sorrowfully went into the closet to get out his old gun, remembering his virgin gun lying somewhere out in the Chesapeake in five feet of salt water. He opened up the case and inside was his new gun instead of the old one. For once, at least, his bungling had paid off.

Later that day, when the storm subsided, we went back to the boat wreck area and found our decoys, boat and motor washed well up into the woods. We recovered everything

*See "Milton and the Three-String Guitar"

except Sluby's old gun. I took the sparkplugs out of my five-horsepower Sea King motor, which only had two more monthly payments due, dumped the salt water, poured in some gas and soon had it running. We headed offshore to where we thought we had gone down and there in a few feet of water was Sluby's gun. Nothing ever seemed to go the way Sluby planned it, although sometimes this was for the better.

In the ensuing years, I gradually began to learn that Long John was somewhat of a local celebrity for his strength and wit in his younger days. I often stopped by to take him some tobacco and discuss old times with him.

One day, after I had raked some hard-shell clams near the area of the wreck, I took a pail of them through the woods to his shack so he could make a chowder. These clams were too big and tough for anything else, but I knew he would turn them into a delicacy.

We sat down on a couple of pine stumps for a chat in the shade. I had heard that my old friend once worked as a stevedore, if you will, loading potatoes at Morley's Wharf. I brought up this subject because Bill Bailey had told me that he knew Long John and he could carry two 175-pound barrels at a time, one under each arm, from the dock up the ramp to the steamboat deck. I had some suspicion about this and mentioned it to Long John in a sort of skeptical way. He took an extra puff from his pipe and, after a pause, condescended to address me again, "Twern't nuttin to it, it was easier to tote two at de time and I don't get no list to de port or starbud." As he told me this he casually and simultaneously crushed a large hard-shell clam in each hand and gave a slight indication of a smile as he watched my reaction from the corner of his eye. He could have made it in show business or basketball or probably anything else, if only. . .

THE ROCKWELL CONNECTION

"Every artist needs an angel."
Robert H. Rockwell

One of the first things I ever wanted to be was a taxidermist. I was irresistibly drawn to wildlife and my idea of a perfect existence was to be closely allied with nature and make a living from it.

It was not long after I had learned to read that I became acquainted with the writings of Carl Akeley, the famous taxidermist, hunter and sculptor of the early 1900's. Actually, the first thing I remember reading was Akeley's account of being attacked by a leopard and running his hand down its throat and killing it. How I wished that a leopard would attack me some day.

Some time later I began to notice advertisements in outdoor magazines for the Northwestern School of Taxidermy's correspondence courses and decided to enroll. I had visions of creating groups of all kinds of birds and animals involved in the eternal conflict between predator and prey, which is, after all, what nature is about.

I enrolled and sent in my money each month and began receiving modest pamphlets explaining various taxidermy projects of increasing complexity. Finally, the pace got too hot for me and as fall approached and my grass-cutting jobs began to drop off I had to resign. I addressed a letter to the Dean and carefully explained my extenuating circumstances. I told him of my hope to resume the course the next spring when the grass grew again. A reply never came and, after this fair notice, I stopped sending my monthly tuition. But the pamphlets kept coming. This delighted me because I was still keen on taxidermy, just short of funds. Then one day the postmaster gave me an envelope from my alma mater containing a bill for my tuition in arrears and a very serious letter explaining that my account would be turned over to a collection agency in Chicago if I didn't pay up right away. So here I was for the first time in my life (not the last) deeply in debt. There was nothing I could do except lie low. And that's what I did all fall and well into winter. Immediately after school each day I hid in the woods, and I kept myself on guard at all times. Finally, I no longer received monthly bills and threatening letters from the taxidermy school. I assumed they had a meeting with their lawyers, executives, and bill collectors and decided that I was not worth pursuing. In the spring, everything was back to normal and I no longer felt like a chased animal. However, I never lost my fascination with taxidermy, and a few years later this interest led me to meet a man who played a major role in my becoming a sculptor.

After working in a shirt factory all day, then cooking supper for the family, my mother went to her evening job at the local theater, where she ran the snack bar. Thus she was in a position to meet lots of people. At some point, she told me that she had gotten to know a man named Robert H. Rockwell who frequently came to the theater with his wife. Mr. Rockwell had recently retired from his position as chief taxidermist for the American Museum of Natural History and had chosen a spot a few miles from my house to spend the rest of his life. This was a tremendous opportunity, and my mother arranged for me to visit the Rockwells.

Often, I have thought of one's path through life as a pinball game. When the ball starts its travel from the top and descends through different guides and past various obstacles, the most minute variation in the beginning will have a profound effect on its final resting place. So it was with me, and if Robert H. Rockwell had chosen another location for his retirement other than the Eastern Shore of Virginia, I probably would have never become a sculptor. Nor would have my son, David.

I will never forget how excited I was walking up the pathway to Mr. Rockwell's house, which strategically over-looked Nassawadox Creek. I was actually going to meet a man who had hunted lions in Africa and bear in Alaska and had mounted the majority of the big game groups in the American Museum of Natural History. Also, as I was to soon learn, he had been along on Carl Akeley's African collecting expeditions.

Mrs. Rockwell graciously met me at the door and ushered me in through a porch decorated with antlers, horns and skulls of the many animals her husband collected on his museum expeditions.

She took me into the living room where Mr. Rockwell was talking with a neighbor. He kindly turned his attention to me and the partially skinned duck I had brought along for his critique. Without hesitation, the world's foremost taxidermist placed the smelly carcass on a beautiful coffee table and proceeded to give me my first live taxidermy lesson. I had been doing everything wrong but instantly memorized all he told me despite my spellbound state.

This first visit merely whetted my appetite for more information, and I was a frequent visitor to the Rockwell household from then on. They always made me feel welcome.

I noticed that Mr. Rockwell spent more time on sculpture than taxidermy and, with his urging, I began to acquire an interest in this medium. He noted this interest and began to encourage me to sculpt small clay models of birds and animals. Taxidermy was a dying art, he said, adding that there was a better future in sculpture.

I carefully followed my mentor's suggestions and soon reached the point in modeling where he encouraged me to make a mold of a small bufflehead duck model I had shaped so I could cast it in earthenware clay and fire the casting.

I tried to remember every word of instruction or criticism he ever uttered to me. Each was a precious gem; and each was carefully picked up and saved and later passed along to my son. Mr. Rockwell's advice covered mechanics, anatomy, design, economics and philosophy. "Don't make hood ornaments." "A good piece of sculpture will roll down a hill." "Always tell a story." "Every artist needs an angel." There were hundreds or perhaps even thousands of these basic rules that were important. Even more important was the intangible inspiration and the beacon that was always there to encourage and guide me.

After the introduction to sculpture through clay came bronze. Mr. Rockwell and I once traveled to New York to the renowned Roman Bronze Foundry to have some of his beautiful horses cast. It was a thrilling experience to walk over the same floors once walked on by Remington, Fraser and Borglum and to watch old Italian craftsmen at work on sculpture of all kinds.

Having a bronze cast in New York was a logistical problem, and this is one reason I later decided to build a foundry of my own. It first entailed getting the model to the foundry intact so a mold and a wax pattern could be made. Then it was a good idea to personally examine the wax pattern before it was cast. Thus, I had the opportunity of traveling to

New York with Mr. Rockwell. This was an experience not to be forgotten.

The foundry was located in a place in New York that was not on Fifth Avenue. I think the name was Corona, and it was quite a bit different from Buzzards' Glory.

The foundry arranged a hotel for us. I guess they didn't have too much choice, and perhaps they didn't realize that it was a welfare hotel with children running up and down the halls all night. After we finally got to sleep, we were awakened early in the morning by screaming in the alley outside our window. However, as it turned out, not many people were maimed or killed on that particular night. In spite of the mid-summer heat, we closed the window and finally got to sleep again. Soon the phone rang. Assuming it was our wake-up call, I simply said thank you and hung up. I was really glad to hear the call, knowing the night was over and we had survived. We washed, shaved, dressed and went down to the lobby. Noticing that it was still dark outside, I looked at my watch and saw it was only three o'clock. Naturally I explored this with the desk clerk on duty and learned that we had been called by mistake. So we went back to sleep in New York City. A few hours later we awoke again. In the relative safety of daylight, we walked to the nearby foundry and spent the day there working on the wax patterns for Mr. Rockwell's horses. It was with some relief that we finished our work and headed home.

Soon after this, I began designing sculpture of my own and had it cast at this foundry. But I always tried to never let the sun set on me in the Big Apple.

Later I used a foundry in Sarasota, Florida, for my castings. On one trip to Florida my flight was canceled in Norfolk due to snow so I was rerouted through Washington, D.C. However, I was a few minutes late and also missed this flight. It was Air Florida 14 which crashed into the Potomac

River on takeoff. I did not learn about this until I finally arrived in Florida. It gave me a queer tingling feeling all over when I heard about this disaster. Before the tingling subsided, I decided to build my own bronze foundry. This was a little after Mr. Rockwell's death, and I always regretted that I didn't get it going in his lifetime. After all, without his encouragement and guidance, I never would have become a sculptor.

NET FISHING

"Let others freeze with angling reeds,
And cut their legs with shells and weeds,
Or treacherously poor fish beset
with strangling snare or windowy net."
                                    John Donne

Of course, you will immediately think fishing with gill nets is unsportsmanlike. It is and it was. But in my youth I had to survive however I could because it was an extreme rarity for me to receive a dividend from a trust or any other kind of handout. Though I respected all wildlife, I caught as many fish as I could and sold them for a profit. I treated them as a crop. If I could dig potatoes faster with a shovel than I could with my hands I used one, and I applied this same logic to fish. I do admit, however, that fishing was much more fun than digging potatoes. Besides, I always heard that Peter and Jesus fished with nets. So if it was proper for them I thought that it would be proper for me, though I am not making comparisons.

Once, while net fishing at night with one of my contemporary friends (I only had about three) along the edge of the Chesapeake Bay, I had an unusual experience which I have not yet fully understood. It was an evening trip with a gill net. On that hot and humid night we caught a few fish but nothing exceptional. Then, as we were taking in the net, a light flashed, seemingly within reach. It appeared to be a ball of fire about the size of a baseball. My first thought was that it was a camera flash, but I realized that neither of us had a camera. Then other flashes occurred, sometimes seconds apart. It was as if a horde of gigantic fireflies were attacking us. We soon realized that this phenomenon was not of our doing in any way and we had no control over it. We tried to leave, but we could not seem to escape this light. Our movement did not affect the relative position of these fascinating, but scary, balls of fire with the boat. Gradually, the flashes diminished and then disappeared entirely.

At first this experience was frightening. However, we soon realized that we were not being harmed, and our fright turned to fascination. For some reason, nature had singled us out for this experience, a tiny speck in an immense body of water being bombarded by balls of light for no apparent reason. I have thought about this occasion often and still have no definite explanation. However, I have read about an electrical phenomenon called St. Elmo's Fire, and I believe this may be the explanation. There must have been a potential electrical condition in the atmosphere which coupled with the right conditions in our boat for a few minutes, and resulted in this eerie display very close to us wherever we went. I have never experienced this since nor have I ever heard of anyone else who has.

This was the only occasion when I had seen fire in the air, but there was frequently 'fire' in the water, as Mitt called it. I am referring to the phosphorescence or chemical glow given off by microscopic animal life, sea nettles and jelly fish. When they were disturbed by an oar, motor, or net, there were times when this phenomenon was so prevalent our net looked like a string of Christmas lights. This yellow-green light could be bright enough to help us see when removing fish from the net.

In the days before nylon came into use, linen or cotton net had to be hung to dry when one got home or it would go through a rot. Mitt called it a 'moon rot', and you would call it spontaneous combustion. Drying the net was a tiresome job after pushing a boat around and handling the net and fish all night, but it had to be done. I devised a large reel similar in appearance to a wheel of a river paddle boat and wound the wet net onto it. This device worked well.

When the net was dry, or we were ready to go fishing again, I just unwound it into a bag or a tub, sometimes mending it as I went or drawing up the holes made by crabs and sharks.

When dry, the slime from sea nettles turned into a fine powder, and, as the net was taken down much of this substance drifted into the air. If you were not upwind, it would get into your noses and cause violent, uncontrolled sneezing. At times, I would take an old piece of net to school with me and shake it out down the halls when no one was looking. The officials of the Health Department never figured out what caused these occasional outbreaks of mysterious sneezing at our school.

The mainstay of our net fishing was fatbacks or jumping mullet.* It was a hard sport to beat. The chasing, stalking, listening, and camaraderie during warm summer

*See "A Bad Night on Machipongo Creek"

nights gave me great pleasure. When alarmed, the fish were fast swimmers. After hearing them (Mitt claimed he could smell them), sneaking up on them, and partially surrounding them with a net, it then became time to be as noisy and conspicuous as possible. We banged on the boat, slapped the water with a pushing pole and flashed our lights on them as they jumped and dove, sometimes "as thick as hair on a dog's back", as Mitt would say. It was a great spectacle to see and hear.

The very opposite of fatbacking in Machipongo Creek in August was fishing for rock (striped bass) in Occohannock Creek in January and February. There was no sound, no chase, no lights, no jumping fish; just an occasional bob of a cork. And it was cold.

One winter in the early fifties, Mitt and I had tried our nets close to Shields Bridge and made a good haul on small rock, about two pounds or so. We first found them in November, and as the winter moved on they became numerous despite our efforts to deplete them.

The local sports fishermen found out about our luck and had great midwinter sport trolling for these game and delicious fish. Then the sports decided that Mitt and I were taking so many fish that we were endangering their recreation and they began to hassle us. Sometimes our nets were cut; then they made us buy a commercial license and the warden began to check us regularly. I think he made it regular because we always gave him a good mess of fish and that put him in a lenient frame of mind. So our fishing continued uninterrupted through February.

We would set out our nets in the evening and fish them once or twice, then go back the next morning and take them up. This was cold work for fingers in wet and freezing late-winter weather. I recall several occasions when we had to take up the net and fish and ice together. We would then go to my friend Burleigh Mears' carpentry shop to sit in front of his large fireplace and remove the fish in comfort.

Finally, the sports gave us a *coup de grace*, and our boat was missing one evening when we arrived to set out our nets. I valued the boat because I had built it myself especially for net fishing and it handled well. I was also emotionally attached to it. Since all of my boats were built by the rack of the eye with no plans, I knew I would never be able to duplicate it.

I always wondered what happened to this boat. About three years later, during an extremely low tide, someone sighted it just below the surface with some concrete blocks in the bottom, and from the description I knew it was mine. I could not summon enough courage to go see it, and it still lies in that same spot, now almost devoured by worms.

If any of you who read this book have information on the culprit(s) responsible for this deed, I will pay a substantial reward.

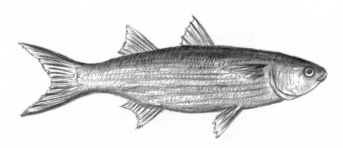

FISHING WITH DYNAMITE

"From our vantage point Edmund Custis' [the author's 17th century ancestor] invention may appear ingenuously simple. As for the curious term 'wreck-fishing,' applied to this invention, one can easily account for it by imagining the devastation produced among large concentrations of fish by underwater explosions."

James B. Lynch, Jr.

At the outset, I want to make it clear that I do not approve of dynamiting fish. It was just one of many such things I did in my youth that I do not condone. Nevertheless, it was exciting, profitable, interesting, and dangerous, so I just could not resist at that stage of my life.

In the 1950's, dynamite was as easy to buy as a candy bar; it just cost a little more. I used to save my grass-cutting money so I could get a few sticks at times. I purchased it from 'Dynamite' Bill Russell whose occupation was dynamiting stumps and irrigation ponds. For the twenty years or so that I knew him, he always carried several cases of dynamite in the trunk of his car. He was a poor driver but fortunately was never involved in an accident.

I had heard tales of his dynamiting fish. My friend, Captain Cabell Mapp, learned the trade from Russell. Then I became involved in this pastime with Cabell.

It was not possible to just go out and successfully dynamite fish anywhere. You had to find them congregated

at certain locations. One such place was called the *Cell.* *
This was a huge concrete and steel structure about five miles
offshore on the eastern side of the Chesapeake Bay in sixty
feet of water. It was built during the war as a ship-degaussing
station to render the ships less susceptible to mines.

In the 1950's the Cell was in a deteriorating state,
partially falling into the water. It was covered with barnacles
and all kinds of marine growth. This attracted myriad little
fish, which in turn attracted large fish. There were sheeps-
head, spadefish, tautog, sea bass, black drum, red drum, and
many other species. It was, and still is to this day, although
now completely under water, a paradise for marine life.

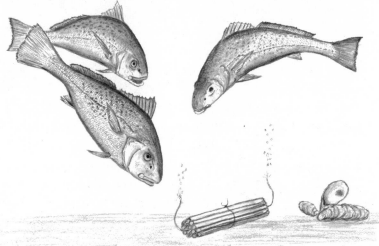

* During the war, Mitt Bundick got a job helping to build this
structure for the government. He had not been on the job long when he
became friends with the supervisor of construction and soon created a
different and less laborious job for himself. I suppose that Chief
Commissarian would be the correct appellation. He was free to come and
go as he pleased as long as he kept the work crew of a hundred or so
supplied with soft crabs, brown eggs, fatbacks, chickens, wild ducks, etc.
Knowing Mitt, I am sure that he not only got his pay check but made
considerable profit furnishing the hierarchy with the delicacies of the
season.

There was really not a lot to dynamiting fish. It took about twenty sticks of dynamite tied tightly together. Two fuses were affixed to two caps and each cap was stuck into a stick of dynamite. Both fuses were lit as insurance in case one of them was extinguished by the water. After both fuses were sputtering menacingly for what seemed to be an eternity, the bundle was thrown into the water. In a few minutes, the concussion of the explosion could be felt on the bottom of the boat. It was as if someone had hit the boat from underneath with an axe. A few seconds later, water would begin to boil up from the depths, along with many fish of all sizes, floating belly up, some still barely alive. We rode around picking them up with a crab net as fast as we could before they could sink again. We would sometimes get over two hundred pounds; some of the spadefish would weigh six to eight pounds, and once in awhile we would catch a big drum fish of forty to fifty pounds. I suppose a lot of fish were killed that never rose to the surface. I have been told that the concussion damaged the fish's air bladder which controlled its buoyancy.

After several expeditions with Cabell, my friend Johnny Johnson and I decided that we would go dynamiting on our own. We took a couple of others with us to show off our prowess in this new sport.

For some reason, we did not make the run to the Cell but instead decided to detonate our twenty sticks of dynamite closer inshore at a spot where we thought there would be fish. The water was much shallower, only about twenty-five feet or so.

Both fuses were lit and we threw the dynamite over. The current was running pretty strong, so we knew in the couple minutes or so it took to explode we would be at least a hundred yards away. We were watching the spot where we threw the dynamite over when suddenly there was a huge explosion right beside our little outboard boat. The boat flew partially into the air, and a huge geyser similar to Old Faithful filled the atmosphere.

We were shaken a bit but unhurt. It did not take us long to figure out what had happened. The current that was pushing us along was also pushing the twenty sticks of dynamite at the same rate and in the same direction.

I know that fishing in this manner was unsportsmanlike, but if I were a fish I guess that I would as soon die of dynamite as I would in a gill net with crabs gnawing at me as I strangled to death.

In defense of our actions, I must say that Captain Cabell was a brilliant conservationist, years ahead of his time. He refused to use more than twenty sticks of dynamite at one time, and somebody ate every fish we took.

SATURDAY NIGHT
ENTERTAINMENT

"In my experience boys are the same in all ages. They don't respect anything, they don't love for anything or anybody."

Mark Twain

I am not sure that the times are right for this story. The times are definitely not right for a re-enactment. The fact that I write about something does not mean that I would want my children or grandchildren, or anyone, in fact, to do some of the things my friends and I did.

Perhaps I should make the excuse that we were misguided, or unguided, youths and created our own entertainment out of boredom. Thus, we were victims of social injustice in that we were not provided with proper forms of recreation to challenge our physical energy and creative minds. Obviously, our government should have pushed wholesome entertainment upon us to foster our minds and bodies for the good of mankind.

In our rural area there were downtrodden minorities that were frequently the butt of our pranks. Actually, when I come to think of it, I am proud to say that we did not discriminate. We played pranks on everyone. It's just that if we had been caught playing these same pranks on our social peers there almost certainly would have been legal and social repercussions. Therefore, we had to be more careful with our jokes on some than others.

There were essentially three of us who masterminded and executed these dastardly deeds. Some did not require much courage and some did; sometimes there is a fine, gray, fuzzy line between courage and stupidity.

First I will tell you about a couple of deeds that did not take a lot of bravery but called for mobility, and this was provided by an old Ford pickup owned by Johnny Johnson's father. Built into this pickup was a condition, I suppose you would call it, which allowed us to trigger an explosion at will. It sounded a lot like a shotgun blast, especially if a set of barrels were pointed at you when you heard it. You see, this old pickup could be made to backfire at any time simply by turning off the ignition while riding along, allowing gasoline to accumulate in the engine and overflow into the muffler and its exhaust, the only way out. Then when the key was turned on again there was a chain reaction of some kind, igniting all the accumulated gasoline with a big bang. Remember, a cupful of gas is equivalent to a stick of dynamite.

Knowing the habits of our victims, we knew that around lunchtime each day there would be several field hands sitting on the benches in front of the local country stores. Usually they were a little drowsy, as there is nothing like a hard morning's work followed by a bottle of soda pop and a bologna sandwich to invite a little midday stupor.

In the truck with us was a double-barreled shotgun. When we were about fifty yards from the store, we cut off the ignition and coasted on. In front of the store we caused several things to happen simultaneously. First a bloodcurdling scream was emitted just to get everyone's attention so they wouldn't miss anything. Then the shotgun was pointed direct-ly at the startled innocents on the benches and the ignition was again turned on with the resulting blast. And so, slumbering, satisfied, sunbathed tranquility was, in a space of about two seconds, turned into a look of certain death authenticated by the attention-getting screams, the emergence of the double-barreled shotgun, and the accompanying blast.

The transformation was immediate, and the survivors (everyone always thought he was the only survivor) clamored to run, dodge, pray and get behind his best buddy on the bench.

We continued on our way while the poor field hands began to look for holes, first in themselves and then in their companions.

In the same vein, one day as we were cruising the back roads on a new gallon of gasoline the three of us had purchased, we were presented with a splendid opportunity. A half-mile or so ahead, peddling peacefully along on his bicycle, was a local bully who had caused us some concern in recent weeks. Of course, we probably would have done the same thing if it had been the preacher's daughter, but on this occasion we felt justified.

Anyway, as we overtook the cyclist, we cut the ignition and stuck the double-barreled shotgun out the window. The proper oath was shouted and then the ignition turned on again with the usual loud explosion. Obviously counting the barrels and the explosion, and figuring that he had escaped the first blast and another was forthcoming, he headed his bicycle for the ditch, the bottom of which was of considerable depth below the water and the briars. As we rode on we could not help but note his thankful look that he had been spared.

In looking back on these misguided escapades in another age, I cannot help but come to the logical conclusion that they made good mufflers in those days.

These preceding deeds required a little timing and nothing else. The last devilment that I will describe (I feel I should not tell you much more along these lines) did require some courage.

In the harvest season our farming area becomes flush with migrant laborers. All week these people work hard in the fields for a pittance, making someone else rich, suffering all kinds of abuse and deprivations. Therefore, on Saturday night/payday, it was time to let all their pent-up frustrations come out. The place to do this was the local minority pool hall. Many people to whom violence was a way of life, if not just a pastime, congregated here Saturday nights. Knifings and shootings were frequent, and alcohol was consumed in large quantities.

One hot Saturday night in August, we decided that a minor explosion in this pool hall would create interesting results. So Hall Ames, Johnny Johnson and I pooled our money, bought a gallon of gasoline, and headed for the town of Exmore. It was easy to tell that we were getting close because of the drunks staggering along the street, and we also met a police car which we figured had been called in to quiet a disturbance. We had an assortment of firecrackers that would have earned the envy of any terrorist. We stopped the pickup truck in front of the den of iniquity as prearranged. There was a mixture of raucous music and screams, curses and shouts emanating from the rickety old building. One person remained in the truck to keep the old engine going. A fat four-inch firecracker was selected from our arsenal and two of us approached the building. The firecracker was calmly lit and the door opened wide, revealing a myriad of red eyes and sweaty faces in the smoke-filled room. Then, when the fuse had burnt to the proper length to allow little time for figuring out what was going to happen, Hall tossed the device into the middle of this mass of humanity on the verge of a surprise. The door was then slammed shut, and I propped two benches against it to delay pursuit and give us better odds for survival. Then we ran to the pickup and cleared the vicinity. As we rode off, the explosion could be clearly heard, but we did not wait to see the probable exodus.

We were so amused that we decided to repeat it again the following Saturday night at the same time. However, we were shrewd enough to not do this a third time because of the obvious possibilities.

In thinking back on these actions and after much agonizing reflection, I must say that I have come to the conclusion that they just don't make good four-inchers any more.

BOAT BUILDING

"There is nothing — absolute nothing — half so much worth doing, as simply messing about in boats."

Kenneth Grahame

My father was a carpenter and a cabinet maker. He had a shop set up in a rented warehouse in the little town of Exmore, about a mile away from our home. He mainly built wooden truck bodies, windows and window frames, and cabinets.

During the summer, weekends, and some evenings, I helped him. As a teenager living in a town of about four hundred, there wasn't much else to do except hunt, fish, and work. Early on, I had been diagnosed as incapable of working with my brain, so it fitted right in for me to work with my hands. After all, if man had not developed an opposing thumb and started using his hands for something other than climbing through the trees, his brain would not have done him much good even if it had developed.

Old man Sam James, who lent my father some money (at two percent interest) to buy tools, decided that he would build a boat, an outboard skiff, in my father's shop. I was delighted that this was going to be done because I was keenly interested in boats, fishing, and the water.

The boat was sixteen feet long and designed for a small outboard motor. It was made of white cedar sides and bottomplanking with white oak ribs, keel, chines*, etc.

After this boat was completed and launched, my father and I decided to build one for us. Ours was patterned after the one the old man had built, and I worked one entire summer to get a five horsepower Sea King outboard motor from Montgomery Ward on the monthly payment plan. Our skiff was flat-bottomed, and before it soaked up a lot of water and collected too many barnacles, it was very fast, about fifteen miles per hour.

About this time, I was tiring of building creosoted truck bodies, window frames and doors, and all those other square things. I decided that 'boat builder' had a better ring to it than 'truck body builder', so I set out to build a boat to sell all on my own with no help from my father or the old man.

I was told that I couldn't build boats, that only certain people of a different and artistic nature could do this. I was determined, however, to get away from creosote, window putty, ninety and one-hundred-eighty-degree angles, and all those mundane things which go with general carpentry. No amount of discouragement could keep me from this goal.

I purchased some lumber from a local professional boat builder, then set up some frames to hold the bent sides in place while the bottom was being nailed on. I had no written plans and used the age-old 'rack of the eye' method for the design. Everything went along fine and while I was building the boat, someone bought it. Then someone else ordered one,

*The timber that connects the sides to the bottom.

and another and another. My boat building business was launched.

In a short period, I was booked up six months ahead of time with orders, allowing about one a week in the summer and one every two weeks during the school term. I experimented with the design, changing the bottom shape gradually until I could guarantee that my boats would do thirty miles per hour with a ten horse power motor. Also, I had read about Henry Ford, so I followed his example in mass production of parts.

I was interested in speed and decided to build a very lightweight hydroplane for myself. My mother gave me an old window shade, and I used this to draw the plans. All of my other boats were built without any plans. But this speedboat needed some careful marine architectural planning, so I drew up the plans, an inch to the foot, and scaled them up when I got into the construction phase. The result was a short, wide, low profile boat with a step in the bottom. As planned, it was very fast, but I miscalculated its turning ability at high speeds, as I was to find out the hard way.

Its trial run was in February, when the waters of the Chesapeake and its tributaries were cold, usually about forty to forty-five degrees.

An older friend, Harry James, loaned me his new twelve-horse Sea King for the maiden voyage. My friend Johnny Johnson, Mr. James, and my father were along for the occasion. I had on my hip boots because of the icy water and put on a life vest at the last minute at someone's insistence, something I never did. Indeed, the boat was very fast. It would skip along at forty miles per hour plus. I was thrilled that all my technology, devised on a curtain shade, was working out as I had planned.

Enjoying being the star of the show, I made several passes in front of the dock and then decided that what the spectators needed was a sharp, high-speed turn. The Sea King was given full throttle and I crouched over the steering wheel, raced by the dock, and came about to the port very quickly; but the boat kept on going in the same direction. The only difference was that it was now sliding sideways over the waves instead of the usual bow-first, stern-last. Suddenly, the side of the boat caught in a wave and I was violently thrown overboard, taking part of the boat with me. The craft kept on without its pilot, designer, builder and owner, making a wide circle and coming back directly at me. I wanted to dive to avoid being hit by the propeller, but the life jacket held me afloat. However, about fifty feet away the pilotless speed boat hit a wave, shot straight up into the air and then landed upside down with the Sea King still roaring for a few seconds.

It was fortunate that I had on a life jacket. My hip boots and heavy clothing made swimming in the icy water impossible. Johnny, seeming to take a purposefully long time, came to pick me up in a rowboat and towed the hydroplane to shore. I didn't feel the cold until I was back at the dock, but I don't think I've ever been colder.

So it was back to the drawing board for me and to dry dock and repairs for the boat. The motor had about as much shock as I did. But we removed the spark plugs and dumped out the salt water and ran it in a barrel of fresh water for an hour and it was as good as new. Can you imagine doing that today to one of the modern outboard motors that has a computer for every function?

Repairs were made to the coaming of the deck, which had come out with me. Soon the boat was ready for another test run. Johnny and I put it into the back of his pickup and launched it again at Shields' Bridge, a concrete structure that crosses Occohannock Creek, near where Mitt and I went net fishing for striped bass in the winter. There was a narrow opening under the bridge and, after feeling things out, I decided to go full speed between the pilings. All pilings are hard, but concrete ones are even more so. I headed for the center of the orifice and had a few feet to spare on each side, but just as I came to the bridge a gust of wind pushed me off course. The boat suddenly slid into the concrete pilings and wound up with a huge hole in one side. I could see that I would sink if I slowed down, so I kept on going, keeping the hole above water until I could turn around and come to rest in the shallows. Now I'm sure you have noticed that Johnny was along on both of the mishaps and undoubtedly was responsible by being bad luck. It certainly had nothing to do with my design or piloting.

I again patched the boat up and this time I sold it. It was entered in several races, and very few people drowned.

Despite this setback, my boat-building business continued to prosper and I was pretty flush for a teenager with no trust fund. The boats cost me about $75 each and I sold them for about $175. I kept several going at one time in all stages of construction.

Once an old farmer traded in a rotten sailboat on one of my new skiffs. The boom, mast, and sail were missing, but Johnny, Hall, and I jerry-rigged the *Kon Tiki*, as we named it, with pine trees for mast and boom and potato sacks for a sail; we had a lot of fun in it. One day, when we were about a mile offshore, the mast came out of the step and tore the deck and port side off when it fell. We sank. It was a long swim in rough weather, but some splinters of wood from the wreck helped us along.

Soon, factory-made boats became popular, and by the time I went to college my business had waned. However, I still had enough to keep me busy, since I had less time for such things while attending the University of Virginia.

I still love to build wooden boats for my sons and grandchildren. There is nothing like the smell of freshly-worked white cedar in the spring, coupled with the cry of the newly arrived laughing gulls. There are not many wooden boats around today; most have been replaced by fiberglass models. And while I hate the look and smell of fiberglass, the upkeep is minimal, a very important consideration in this age of haste.

TECHNICAL ADVANCES

At the University of Virginia, I majored in Anthropology and studied a lot about how innovations introduced into a culture effected changes, some good and some bad. It was then that I began to think about how certain technical innovations caused changes in the culture in which I lived.

Monofilament nylon, when it first appeared on the market in the early 1950's, was what I, at that time, considered a real breakthrough if one were attempting to wrestle a living from the Chesapeake Bay.

I was introduced to monofilament line by my old friend Cabell. He had ordered a spool of it from Sears Roebuck and Co. when he got their spring catalog. As you may have noticed from other stories in this book, Cabell liked to play jokes on humans as well as nature. When he unwrapped his package of line, the first thing he did was pump some water into a dish pan and immerse about a foot of it. He noticed that it practically disappeared. I suppose it was then that he got his inspiration for a little fun.

We got into his car and went down to the head of

Occohannock Creek where it narrows into a gut and meanders through a marsh. This happened to be a favorite feeding ground of the black skimmer. Now, these birds feed differently from most; they fly just above still water with their lower beak cutting through the surface. Whenever they run up on a minnow, they automatically close their mouth on the prey. The lower beak is a little longer than the upper, and I understand that this is the only sea bird in the world in which this is true.

We tied a piece of the new line to an old pine root just below the surface. Then we stretched the line across the gut to another root on the opposite side. We then hid behind the pine stump and waited. Evening approached, and this is the favored fishing time for skimmers because it's usually when surface water is calmest and many little fish feed close to the surface. Some of these birds soon appeared, flying gracefully along with their lower beaks in the water. They approached the unseen obstruction just below the water's surface, and the lead bird caught a minnow just a few feet before it crossed the line. It retracted its fishing gear momentarily and crossed the monofilament safely. Just behind it were two others. Simultaneously they encountered the line with their lower beaks and both were upended instantaneously. We were greatly amused at the terror of the two unfortunate (but unhurt) birds that had just fallen victim to modern technology. Birds learn quickly, however, and we could repeat this only a few more times before the skimmers decided to search for minnows elsewhere. Recently I sat on this same old pine stump and watched the sun set over the Chesapeake. The birds no longer fish here because most of the fish are gone. Cabell is gone, too.

A better example of how monofilament affected my life and my culture is shown by the advent of its use in fish net. My first nets were cotton and linen, both of which would rot quickly if not given loving care. By care, I mean that they must be dutifully dried after each use and all holes mended regularly. I was taught to mend nets by my old friend, Ray Shackleford, gone long ago. He was a purist who made his own mending needles, carved from holly or dogwood.

"A stitch in time saves nine" was our local saying that applied to fish nets. Now the well-informed all over the world use this phrase. And it was true that it was better to mend your net the following day after a night's fishing. As Captain Ray taught me, the hole was trimmed to two flats and all the rest points, and one started with a flat and ended with a flat and your net was mended. Nylon multifilament net actually was on the market before monofilament. It was much stronger and needed less care than linen or cotton and wouldn't go through a moon rot, but just as cotton and linen did, these nets made quite a statement to fish in water during daylight, making night fishing a necessity. However, monofilament net practically disappeared in the water and made night fishing unnecessary. If your net got opaque-looking, all you had to do was put it in a barrel of water with a little bleach and it became transparent again. Also, this new and better net eventually became so cheap that it didn't pay to mend it. This was a good thing because it was difficult to tie knots with monofilament nylon. (As I write this, I'll bet that I'm one of very few men left on the Eastern Shore who can mend a net. Net-menders are no longer a part of our culture.)

Before my time local people in the winter months wove their own nets from balls of twine. Then, just as cheap monofilament put the local net-menders out of business, factory-made linen and cotton nets put the local net-maker out of business.

The big impact that monofilament net made upon my life was the freedom from fishing at night. This allowed me to spend more time at night hunting raccoons, bullfrogs, 'possums and other things after my voice changed.

One of my first monofilament nets was designed for large fish (thirty to eighty pounds). Webby Martin, my net-fishing expert friend who also had a new net, and I were very eager to try them out in the daytime. So one spring afternoon we tied our new nets together and strung them out across the tide near a sand bar on the edge of the Chesapeake.

We were hoping to catch either a black or a red drum (channel bass). These fish migrated up the Bay in the spring, looking for their spawning grounds. They become quite large, with some blacks going up to one hundred pounds.

We were full of hope with our new state-of-the-art fish net as we stretched out about two hundred yards of it in four to six feet of water. No sooner had we got it all out when several of the corks began to bob up and down as big fish became entangled and gilled. We just sat back for awhile and watched the spectacle, counting our money and planning how to spend it. What a cultural impact this new monofilament was going to make on our lives: cars, girls, shotgun shells, outboard motors and, of course, more and more monofilament net.

When we figured that we had made enough money, we went to the downtide brail* and pulled it out of the sand to begin the task of hauling the net into the boat and getting out our prizes. Oh, we were such good fishermen! Here we were in the right spot at the right time. We knew where big fish would be traveling, and we were waiting for them with the latest gill-net technology. This was a deadly combination: savvy watermen and good equipment.

---

* A pole at each end of a gill net which is pushed into the mud to hold the net. Usually just a sapling cut from the woods.

As we began to pull in the net, one of us on the lead line* and one on the cork line**, we could immediately feel the surge of big fish struggling to get free of the monofilament line caught in their gills. The first fish we came to was not a prized drum but a lowly and worthless stingray. The net had done a great job of entangling its stinger, a sharp four-to-six-inch spear-like bony protrusion at the base of its tail. This is a formidable weapon. It is needle-sharp and covered with many small barbs set in reverse so that once imbedded in something they will firmly hold this vicious armament in place. And if this were not enough, this whole thing is covered with a poisonous slime which results in an almost immediate infection if it pierces one's skin. In truth, it is mainly a defensive mechanism. If you do not step on the stingray or irritate it in some way, such as catching it in a gill net, it will cause you no problem.

The ray was firmly caught by its stinger because all the little reverse barbs had entangled on every strand of monofilament it touched. It was an awful job to separate the ray from the net without damaging the latter. We could, of course, just cut the net away from the stinger. This would have been quick, but it would have created a big hole in our precious new nets. So we persevered until we had untangled the net and its undesirable catch; both were unharmed. I do not think that we considered this ray to be anything other than an accidental stray until we came to another almost immediately. It was then that we remembered that these stingrays come up the Bay in vast schools at this time of year, along with the drum fish. We went through the same time-consuming procedure, and when we came to the next ray only a few feet down the line we knew three things: one, that the

* The line that holds one edge of the net down.

**The line that holds the other edge up.

monofilament was very efficient at catching in the daytime; two, that we had probably caught a world's record haul of stingrays; and three, we would be there for at least two tides disentangling them.

Dejected, we decided that we could get the rays out of the net quicker if we pulled them up on the sand bar, now exposed by the falling tide. We anchored our boat and pulled the entire net onto the sand. At the same time, by getting the net out of the water, it could not catch any more of these awful creatures that were so hard on our hands and our egos. There were so many in the net I do not believe there was room for any more.

This task took the rest of the ebb and most of the flood tide. We learned a very hard lesson. To this day, I do not set a net without giving some thought and consideration to the whereabouts of any rays that may be in the area.

It is claimed by some that ray and skate fins taste like scallops. In the fishing industry I understand that it is common practice to use a pipe-like device to punch out cylinders of the white meat for sale as scallops. Once, at a party in England, I was talking with a chap who told me he had just had a jolly good day of fishing. When I naturally inquired about the nature of his catch, he proudly admitted that it consisted entirely of skate. I replied, "That's bloody good."

They are a powerful and sporting fish to catch on a rod and reel, but, for the most part, fishermen in the U.S. try to avoid them. However, during their spring foray into the Chesapeake they will take the hook so readily and they are in such tremendous numbers that they make it almost impossible to fish for anything more worthy.

I once took my youngest son, Bob, when he was about eight years old, to an area of the Bay shore where a few red drum (channel bass) had been recently caught. As this area was accessible by automobile, the shore was lined with dozens of eager anglers. It was spring, the time of the year when rays make their appearance. As he and I walked down the shore past myriad anglers, looking for a spot to fish, we passed several fishermen catching rays. The shore was strewn with them, discarded by the frustrated drum fishermen. Finally, we found a spot with space enough between other anglers for my son to make a cast. No sooner had his peeler crab bait hit the water than it was grabbed by something, quite likely a ray. He fought this fish for about thirty minutes. I did not take much interest in the outcome because I naturally expected it to be a ray. Finally, he got the denizen close. I was about ready to cut it loose when it broke the surface exposing a row of beautiful bronze scales, shining in the setting sun. I proudly helped Bob land a thirty-pound channel bass. We unhooked the fish and he was ready to take it home to show his older brothers, so we retraced our steps amid the envious anglers and thrashing rays. I often wonder how they felt at seeing one child, one cast, one drum beached while they were inundated by rays.

ALASKAN EXPEDITION

"Oh the North Countree is a hard countree
That mothers a blood brood;
And its icy arms hold hidden charms
For the greedy, the sinful and lewd."
                    Edward E. Paramore, Jr.

After hearing my mentor, Robert Rockwell, talk about his adventures in Alaska and then reading his autobiography, I decided that I had to go there someday. Finally, my friend Bagley Walker and I were on our way.

I particularly wanted to collect certain specimens to use as reference material in my porcelain sculpture of birds. Therefore, before signing up for this trip, I obtained assurance from our wildfowl guide, Mike Utecht of Cold Bay, Alaska, that the area abounded in Steller's eider, emperor geese, and harlequin ducks.

We allowed time for a visit to Anchorage before heading southwest to Cold Bay. On the flight to Anchorage, we met an oil driller who loaned us a cabin in this area.

We had expected to see herds of caribou, vast flocks of geese and ducks, and other wildlife but found the area to be very sterile, almost devoid of life. We drove several miles to a bird sanctuary, and I believe I saw more birds in my back yard the morning I left Virginia than I did in the entire Anchorage area.

After a few days, we boarded the plane for our flight to Cold Bay. That's when the fun began. I had heard and read about bad weather being responsible for many airline crashes in this area, and I was a little apprehensive. As we neared Cold Bay, the weather became increasingly treacherous. When we reached the airport, our plane circled and circled while I anxiously looked down, hoping to see a runway beneath the fog and rain. I assume the pilot was doing the same thing. Finally, there was a small hole through all this soup, and the ground came into view with an airliner wreckage in its center. I later learned that the frequent wrecks are just pushed aside because the area's remoteness does not encourage salvage. Of course, I was convinced that this wreck had just occurred and was one of several that day and that we were circling, waiting our turn to take a chance. We managed to land safely, and Mike, our famous waterfowl guide, and his Chesapeake Bay retriever met us. It made me feel right at home to see this breed of dog so far from the Bay.

Mike's home overlooking the Bering Sea was not far from the airport, and in a few minutes he had delivered us to his cabin. As we walked onto his porch, the first thing I noticed was a large hole about chest-high, through the wooden door panel. When questioned, he explained that a few nights before a bear had been trying to get in so he had shot through the door to scare it away. Apparently unharmed, the bear retreated. Mike's home was to be our base of operations for a couple of days before we went out to his remote 'wildfowl' cabin on an island about fifteen miles away.

We did not have time that day to do any hunting because it was already late, but my hopes ran high for the next day, and I anticipated blinds, decoys, hunting gear, and waterfowl in abundance.

The next morning I awoke filled with excitement and began to try to talk to Mike about his duck hunting. It didn't take long for me to realize that Alaska's greatest waterfowler had never seen a decoy and had no blinds. I also learned that he just didn't quite feel up to hunting that day so he was going to sit by the stove. However, being the great guide that he was, he magnanimously loaned us his truck so we could explore the island. We took our guns and shells and set off alone.

Bagley and I had noticed some emperor geese on the beaches, so we parked the truck and tried stalking them as they ate the seaweed that had been washed up. We succeeded in bagging a few of these beautiful birds, and I took them back to Virginia and used them for reference material for years. But despite our success I felt we deserved the luxury of being guided.

The next day we convinced Mike to actually take us duck hunting (after all, that is why we hired him). So the three of us and the Chesapeake Bay retriever climbed into Mike's old truck and traveled about twelve miles to a beautiful area of hilly tundra with a stream running through it. There were a few ducks flying around. Unfortunately, these were not the Harlequins and Steller's eiders I wanted for my porcelain waterfowl studio. They were mallards, just like we had in the Virginia marshes. At least we were duck hunting, even if we had no decoys and no boat. After a long wait behind some rocks beside the dead-salmon-littered stream, a flock came by and one bird was in range. I shot him and he fell into the middle of the stream, which would have prevented us from retrieving him if we had not been lucky enough to have Mike's fully-trained duck dog to solve this problem. Before the duck had hit the water, the dog was bounding forth to retrieve it, or at least I thought he was going to retrieve it. Actually, *take possession* would be a more appropriate phrase because what he did was grab the bird and go to the other side of the stream and commence to dine on duck. No amount of hollering had any effect on him, and he did not return to our side until nothing was left of the carcass except a few feathers. Mike had a little talk with him and assured us this would not happen again. In awhile another duck was shot, this time closer to our side, and I ran to get it. However, just before I could put my hand on the bird the dog charged past me, grabbed the duck, swam to the other side, and quickly ate it also. This discouraged us from further hunting. You must admit that this dog was smart because he obviously knew that he could swim to the far side of the stream and enjoy his meal in peace.

On the way home I reminded Mike that one of my goals on this expedition was to collect a harlequin duck. Mike agreed to show them to me. He drove to a harbor where I could look offshore and see some little specks that he assured me were harlequins. He was just technically keeping his part of the bargain.

The next day, Mike's assistant arrived. (He was a friendly Indian whose name I have forgotten, but he did not speak with a forked tongue.) We at last prepared to take Mike's boat to his camp on one of the many islands in this part of the Bering Sea.

The trip was interesting because of the wildness of the area, with seals abundant and several species of birds always in view. The sand of the beaches was pure black because of its volcanic origin, and the tide raced past the little islands at tremendous speed, at least eight knots. I was elated to see an abundance of diving ducks along the way, but they were in such an advanced degree of moult that they were flightless and indeed had so few feathers that I could not identify them.

After this interesting ride of an hour or so, we arrived at Mike's wilderness camp. It was a metal building of the Quonset design and set on the high part of an island of several hundred acres with gentle hills covered with lichens and flowers and no trees, true tundra.

When we arrived at the one-room metal shack, it was apparent that it had been under stress of some kind because several sheets of metal had been ripped off. Mike did not seem surprised and said that bears did this every year. The tremendous strength of the bears was evident; marks from their claws deeply scarred the metal, and the two by four framework was shattered in places as if it were match sticks.

I reminded Mike that I really wanted to collect some Steller's eiders, a beautifully colored and marked bird. That was one of the main reasons we were making this trip. He shyly told me that we had already seen many eiders. They were the molting ducks we had encountered on the way out.

So here I was, literally at the end of the earth, with my life savings spent on a collecting expedition primarily for harlequins and eiders, the former so far offshore that they were not even in rocket range, and the latter in moult. Mike seemed to feel that he had kept his part of the bargain so he and his Indian 'guide', who did not know a duck from a gull, set about repairing his lodge. It seemed to me that the Indian was suspiciously more of a carpenter than a guide, and the lodge looked more like a bear-hunting facility than a duck hunting facility. And it seemed that Mike anticipated that the lodge would need repairs before the opening of bear season. So, instead of being on a first-class duck-hunting trip with Indian guide and white duck hunter, we were just incidental passengers who, for a fee, were allowed to go along on a routine lodge patch-up job.

Bagley and I were disturbed and felt we had been conned to a certain degree. Here we were in a beautiful wilderness with no transportation, no telephones, no lawyers, and no police. All we could do was entertain ourselves for three days while the lodge was being repaired by Mike the duck hunter/bear hunter and his Indian guide/carpenter.

However, while they were working, we had a good time roaming the island, expecting to see a brown bear around every corner and creeping up on ducks and geese that landed in the tundra. We did not get any birds near the water, but the undulating hills and tundra flowers were good cover for stalking when we saw small flocks land, always out of sight into a depression or the flowers.

On one of my little unguided forays I found a hole in the top of a hill about six to ten feet wide and three feet deep with numerous whale ribs lying about. It was apparent that this was someone's home a long time ago.

At last our time was up and, with the tides and the weather right, Mike announced that we were to leave after lunch. No eiders and no harlequins would leave with us.

Being a staunch believer in some parts of the Old Testament, I had in the recesses of my mind a little simmering about "an eye for an eye and a tooth for a tooth" and how this should legitimately apply to Mike. Bagley was not so deeply religious, or vindictive, so it was left to me to settle the score. In these situations I am a firm believer that the Lord will provide. He did.

We were all sitting around eating our last meal at the freshly repaired lodge when it hit me like a bolt from heaven.

Mike announced in an authoritative way that we should be careful not to spill a crumb lest the bears detect them with their keen noses and then tear the metal off the sides of the building, hoping to find a cache of food.

I was careful to do exactly as instructed; however, as he left the lodge with a load of repair tools, I acted. I grabbed a can of sardines and opened them, emptying the contents between a mattress and its covers. Mike soon reappeared and announced that we were ready to return to Cold Bay. By this time, the lodge smelled like an Eastern Shore fish packing house in peak season. I really didn't expect the smell to permeate the place so quickly and was afraid that he would notice it. I actually think, from the slightly quizzical expression on his face, that Mike may have caught wind of it. He was in a hurry to get away with the tide though, and I distracted him by pointing out a nonexistent sea otter and at the same time mentioning that there was a big dead salmon down on the shore that was causing a stink.

We loaded our gear into the boat, started the motor, and were soon racing along with the current, close to the beautiful black sand beaches. As we rounded a bend in the meandering tidal stream, we came close to a huge brown bear which practically ignored us. It was standing on its rear legs, towering about eight feet in the air, with its nose turned toward the lodge. It seemed to be sniffing the downwind breeze. I have no further information on this matter.

A BAD NIGHT ON
MACHIPONGO CREEK

"In converse be reserved, yet not morose,
In season grave, in season, too, jocose."
Benjamin Franklin

To get the thread of this little story, it is necessary for the readers to familiarize themselves with certain technical words of the net-fishing trade.

brail - a pole that is at each end of a gill net and pushed into the mud to hold the net, usually just a sapling cut from the woods.

drag anchor - any object such as a brick or piece of metal with a rope tied to it that will not dig into the bottom and hold, but will drag along as the net is pulled into the boat.

shirk - a vicious fish - there are several varieties: great white, tiger, dog, sand, thresher, etc. Often, in certain localities, they are misnamed shark.

cat-tongue oyster - a group of young oysters, all growing together in a clump with sharp bills, resembling a bunch of razor blades embedded in concrete.

pinhead croakers - the adolescent young of the croaker. About 6 to 8 inches long and not big enough to eat. They have needle-sharp fins and gill covers as hard and sharp as knives.

fatback - a vegetarian, surface-feeding fish of many subspecies, erroneously called mullet in other parts of the world.

kinnoo - a boat carved out of a large pine tree; not to be confused with a canoe.

rock - has nothing to do with geology but is a mound of oyster shells and live oysters, usually exposed at low tide.

creek - a large tidal inlet that may be a mile wide and several miles long. Not to be confused with creeks in other parts of the country which some people call cricks but should properly be called branch or a ditch.

gut - a smaller tributary leading into a main body of salt water. It has nothing to do with anatomy.

moon rot - a process similar to spontaneous combustion that can affect a net or a pile of fish whether the moon is out or in.

Now, the story:

Mitt and I had been working on a big run of fatbacks for several nights in August and we were catching four hundred to six hundred per night and peddling them for a dollar a dozen. We were getting rich and having a good time (a good combination). Fatbacking was one of my favorite sports because there was the element of the chase involved. We used nets but did not just put a net into the water and leave it for fish to blunder into. We actually stalked and chased and corralled these fish, putting the net overboard and taking it up repeatedly as opportunities came and went.

The way it worked was to pole along quietly until you heard a school of fish jumping, then maneuver your boat very quietly downtide from them, put the brail out and do a semicircular maneuver around them as quickly as possible. After the net was out, usually twenty to thirty fathoms, and the last brail was down, the action began. Fatbacks would be jumping everywhere, including into the boat; sometimes they would hit us in the face or get into our boots. Now, the more noise we made the better, so we beat our pole on the water and on the boat and turned on our flashlights so the fish would become frantic and end up gilled in the net. When they were all scared away or had been gilled, the net was pulled onto the stern of the boat and the fish had to be removed from the net with a deft twist and push movement.

Fatbacks are torpedo-shaped fish, and while they start out as fingerlings in the spring, by July they are about eight to ten inches long and can be caught in a gill net with one-inch mesh (an inch square). At this stage, it takes about two to make a pound. Later in the season, we would switch to a one and one-eighth inch net and they would weigh about a pound each. We couldn't increase the price much because everybody was getting tired of fatbacks by then. Besides, we had been selling them by the dozen and not by the pound. Then when hog killing season came, people took advantage of that for a change of epicurean delights. So all of these facts adversely influenced the fatback market late in the season. However, we did get some orders for a few washing tubs full from some old timers with the vision to salt some down for winter.

On this night, our mutual friend, Captain Cabell Mapp, had asked to come along to join in the fun. Cabell didn't need the money because he had a high school diploma and was captain of a steamship, but he was a keen outdoor sport. We knew he would be in the way and was notorious for playing jokes on people and probably would eliminate the possibility of this outing's being a successful financial endeavor. We had already saturated the market for the time being, and, with a weekend coming up, we knew that all of our customers would be into ribs and greens for a couple of days. Besides, we were going primarily for the sport. We put our nets, tubs,

Coca-Colas, brails, lights, and Mitt's new drag anchor (a rusty old starter from a junked Model T Ford) into our old log kinnoo and pushed off just as the last light faded.

We had not gone far when Cabell insisted he heard fatbacks jumping. Mitt and I disagreed and we kept on. Cabell continued to claim that we were in a big school of fatbacks so finally Mitt pushed the first brail into the mud and the net slid off the stern until it was all gone and the last brail was stuck in an oyster rock. Right away we knew we had not set on fatbacks because none were jumping. They frantically jump several feet in the air when surrounded by a net. The net was bobbing and surging, however, and we knew something was in it.

Immediately we picked up the downtide brail and threw over the drag anchor to keep the boat from drifting over the net as we pulled it in. We soon saw that we should not have listened to Cabell just because he graduated from high school. Our net was full of pinhead croakers, commercially valueless and very difficult to remove from the net. Each one had to be backed out of the net and could not be shoved through the openings, as one can do with fatbacks. We received a multitude of cuts from the razor-like gills and many punctures from the needle-sharp fins. It was a time-consuming job. Plus, the longer the net was left in the water with fish in it, the more crabs came to eat the fish. Then the shirks came, attracted by the crab-bitten fish. All Cabell did was admire how well the drag anchor worked and left all the work to Mitt and me.

I think Mitt knew that they were the wrong brand of fish before we set on them. But he wanted to teach Cabell a lesson and overdid it. It was an awful mixture of cut fingers, fish slime, mosquitoes, jimmy crabs, and small shirks tearing holes in the net. The holes were particularly disturbing to me because I was the only one who knew how to mend them; I knew I would have a job to get the net back in shape. It took so long to get all the fish out, with the croakers and crabs all tangled up, that part of the net, piled up on the stern of the boat almost went through a moon rot. Mitt happened to think of it in time, let out some of the heat, and poured some water on it.

Finally, all the net was in, including many new holes. Mitt blamed this on Cabell, who insisted that the tears would just let the grass through and actually improve the net. To quiet Mitt down, Cabell complimented him on the drag anchor as he pulled it in. Mitt explained that it was just a junk Model T starter but agreed that it worked perfectly, holding the boat back just enough to keep it from running up over the net as it was being pulled onto the stern.

It was now about midnight and we hadn't caught one fatback. We really didn't need any because, as I have said, we had flooded the market earlier in the week. Mitt wanted to catch a bunch anyway. I suppose he was like the prostitute who, when asked what she did for recreation after she got off from work, replied that she had sex.

We pushed along, listening for jumping fatbacks. Mitt had to ask Cabell to cut off his flashlight because the light would spook the fish before we could surprise them. Cabell had been using his light to minutely inspect the old rusty Model T starter.

We finally heard some fatbacks jumping around an oyster rock right at the mouth of a gut a few boat lengths out into the main creek. We carefully stalked the school of fish. When close enough, we put out the brail and ran out the net, beat on the water, banged on the washing tub, and the fatbacks bolted toward the net, some jumping into it and the lucky ones jumping over it.

When all the fish had either left the scene or had been gilled, Mitt asked Cabell to throw over the drag anchor. After

166

looking at it and scratching off some rust and mud, he finally dropped it over the side. At this point, Mitt was showing some sign of irritation over Cabell's interest in the improvised anchor, but he remained quiet.

We began to pull in the net with a lot of fatbacks, so Mitt got into a better mood. Soon the jimmy crabs began to clamp onto the fatbacks, an oily fish and very good crab bait. Mitt and I took out the fish as fast as we could. In those days each of us could keep one in the air all the time. Now I'm much slower, I guess because my fingers are so important to my work. From time to time we pulled up an entangled crab that wouldn't let go. However, this didn't hold us up for long because Mitt just gave the crabs a couple of blows with the ball of his fist and this sort of pulverized them. Then we could shake them out of the net in pieces. Cabell was supposed to be holding the light on the net so we could see what we were doing, but he kept shining it down in the water on the drag anchor. Mitt was a little irritated but kept on taking out fish and pounding crabs. He pulled up onto the stern what he thought was a big crab and gave it two big whacks with his fist before he could stop. Then he cursed out in pain. Cabell took his light off the drag anchor and on the stern of the boat was a cluster of cat-tongue oysters covered with Mitt's blood. Cabell promised to do a better job with the light, and we finally got all the fish out.

We decided to make one more set because Cabell wanted some fish to salt down for the winter. We pushed on, listening for mullet. Periodically, Cabell would turn on his light and carefully look at the Model T starter as if he were picking fleas off of his bird dog. Mitt could finally take it no longer, and he put down his pushing pole, crammed some tobacco into his pipe with the nub of his shot-off finger, took a puff, thought awhile, and asked the question that had slowly entered his mind, "Cabell, why are you looking at that damned anchor?"

This is what Cabell had been working toward all night. He replied, "Well Mitt, I'm looking for a part number; your starter does such a good job I'm going to order one like it from the Ford Motor Company."

Mitt made no reply but just turned the kinnoo around and headed home. We didn't catch Cabell's fish to salt down for the winter.

PIRATES FROM THE NORTH

"Behold, a people cometh from the north country, . . . They are cruel and have no mercy; their voice roareth like the sea. . ."

Jeremiah, Chapter 6, verses 22 and 23

Cabell was really a bad influence on me. Besides dynamiting fish, which they say is illegal, he got me into the practice of hunting out of season. One day in March in the early 1950's, he and I were shooting red-breasted mergansers on the Chesapeake Bay when we had a brush with the law.

It is good to go duck hunting in March when the season has long been closed and the air is beginning to warm up. Most of the ducks have gone north by then, but there are always a lot of 'shell ducks' around at that time, especially along the shores of the Bay. They are pretty birds at this time of the year, and they will stool to anything. I have even seen them decoy to half a grapefruit dumped overboard by some of those northern yachts that migrate up and down the Bay. These ducks, being of the saw-tooth merganser type, live off small fish and are therefore very fishy-tasting birds. Many people will not eat them for this reason. This never made any sense to me. I always liked the taste of fish, whether it were in a duck or a fish, especially in March when I haven't had any fish since October.

On this day, Cabell and I had bagged several beautiful birds. We were sitting on the sandy shore near our anchored boat, talking about the coming fishing season, when we heard the distant drone of an airplane. It got our attention, and soon a low-flying seaplane came into view. Right away we figured it was up to no good. The plane flew right over us and spotted our boat and a few decoys that we still had out, and I suppose they figured that we were up to no good. I guess all of us were correct, depending on your perspective. Anyway, the seaplane made a turn while we grabbed our decoys. We started our outboard motor and began to make a run for our harbor, which was a little inlet about a half-mile away near the mouth of Occohannock Creek. But the seaplane was too quick for us. It was apparent that its crew was going to land right beside us and board our boat. At the last minute we realized we had a chance if we could get to a nearby out-of-season fish trap, and we headed for it.

Now at this time of year the fish traps have no net in them and there remains only a line of poles about two hundred yards long. Each pole is about four inches in diameter and sticks out of the water several feet. More importantly, they are spaced about ten feet apart, and this seaplane had a wingspan that looked to be about twenty-five feet or so. Had the tide been high, the wings would have gone over the tops of the poles. But the Lord was looking out for us, and the tide was down low enough so that the wings would hit the top of the poles. The tide was still falling, so it would be a long time before the plane could get over them.

They were determined to get us after we refused to surrender, so they gunned the motor and went all the way around the end of the poles to get on the same side as we were. However, since there was no net between the poles we just pushed over to the opposite side where the seaplane had been moments before. We did this a few times, and finally they cut their motor and tried to convince us to give up. Holding up their identification for us to see, they identified themselves as federal game wardens.

They announced that they would appreciate it greatly if we would allow ourselves to be arrested and have our ducks and guns and boat and motor confiscated. We explained to the wardens that we couldn't see that far because we had forgotten our glasses, and we didn't know who they were. (Neither of them took a good photo.) We also explained that they could be after stealing our guns or something. They even wanted us to move the potato sacks that happened to be hanging over the bow, obscuring the license numbers on our boat. I told them that these numbers were very old and had not been renewed for years because each year we didn't think the old boat would last another season and they probably were illegible so there wasn't any sense in moving the bags so they could view expired numbers.

This seemed to irritate them further, and they again gunned their plane around to our side of the poles in frustration. We simply pushed over to the opposite side again. This went on for about a half-hour or so, and I guess they were getting short of petrol because they finally left us in a roar of the engine and a lot of spray. The plane took off heading south and saluted goodbye with a sporting wave of its wings.

We watched them fly out of sight and then raced toward our harbor and made it safely with no further trouble with Northerners trying to steal our guns that day.

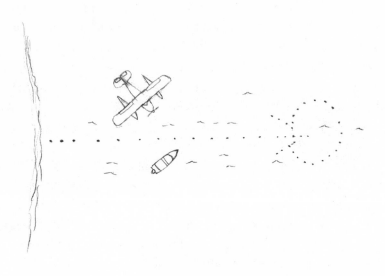

CABELL, SLUBY AND
THE OYSTER TONGER

"Oh, East is East, and West is West, and never the twain shall meet,
Till Earth and Sky stand presently at God's great Judgment Seat;
But there is neither East nor West, Border, nor Breed, nor Birth,
When two strong men stand face to face, though they come from the ends of
the earth!"

Rudyard Kipling

There was a strong westerly breeze going that day on the Chesapeake in the summer of 1840. All the sailboats were enjoying it and headed north and south with 'bones in their mouths'. As usual, sails dotted the horizon in every direction.

Everything was normal for just about everyone except my great-grandfather, John Thomas Turner. He was nine years old and was drifting eastward before the wind in a small rowboat. His point of embarkation that morning was Glouce-ster. No one knows if his trip across the Chesapeake were intentional or accidental. Nevertheless, he floated up on Tangier Island and lived there for many years. He married a local girl and they lived on Nannie's Marsh. He eventually had his own boat and crew and earned the non-military title of Captain.

I do not know much about him, and most of what I do know I learned from one of my Medical College of Virginia professors, Dr. Willie Crockett. Dr. Crockett's mother's father was adopted and raised by Captain John and his wife. Perhaps this is why they decided to let me have a degree.

Tangier Island is a speck of a few hundred acres in the middle of the Chesapeake Bay and inhabited by about one thousand English descendants. Almost all make a living from the water. It is a hard life of crabbing, fishing and oystering. Most of their lives are spent on Tangier. Although, at times, these hardy people are seen (and heard; they have a distinct Elizabethan accent) on the mainland of the Eastern Shores of Virginia and Maryland.

With all this in mind, we can now move ahead to a day in the fall of 1951 when Cabell, Sluby, and I were busy putting up a duck blind, getting ready for the coming water-fowl season. After a hard morning's work, we decided to go to the local diner for lunch. We thought this might be better fare because the last time we had lunch at one of my partners' homes, his wife (I won't say which one since they are both still living) had tired of preparing lunch for us and gave us all dog food sandwiches. They weren't bad. But when we learned their true nature, we no longer patronized that establishment. I assume this was the desired effect. Anyhow, on this day at the diner we and a few other men lined up before the waitress and placed our orders. I forget exactly what we ate except that it was not dog food sandwiches. Cabell and Sluby each had a beer.

Cabell always liked to play jokes* and Sluby was one of his favorite victims. I think this was because of Sluby's inherent susceptibility to being the butt of a joke. He never seemed to realize that he was a jokestee and never attempted to be the jokester. Actually, all you had to do was hang around Sluby a little while and he would play a joke on himself.** Cabell had sized up the situation and decided that it was an opportune time for a prank on Sluby. Cabell played

*See "A Bad Night on Machipongo Creek"

**See "Boatwreck on the Chesapeake"

a joke on someone almost every day, but for some reason he never tried one on me.*

Cabell noticed the two men sitting beside us; an old man sitting next to Sluby and a younger man, his companion, next to him. Cabell could instantly evaluate any situation and, as expertly as a playwright from New York, initiate a sequence of events which could be precipitated in the future to a conclusion for his own amusement and someone else's detriment.

The man next to Sluby was old, small, and weathered. His skin was so wrinkled that he looked like one of those liposuctioned sun worshippers from Palm Beach. He clearly mirrored a lifetime spent battling nature as he tried to wrestle a living from the Chesapeake. He was a waterman, no question about it. He also ordered a beer.

His companion was a robust young man, deeply tanned, and obviously someone who spent most of his life outdoors. Clearly it was not playing polo or golf. His shoulders were broad and his arms were well-muscled. Not an ounce of fat showed under the weathered skin of his six-foot-three-inch, two-hundred-twenty-pound body. It was apparent he had spent much time either working out in a gym or tonging oysters. All things considered, it was quite probable that it was the latter. Both men had on hip boots rolled down past the knee and both were obviously from Tangier Island, out in the Chesapeake Bay.

After a few beers, the old man had to go to the men's room. Upon his return, Sluby followed suit. It was now time

* It is only now that I have finally realized why I was never on the receiving end of one of his jokes. I think this was because I was capable of building boats, sticking duck blinds, carving decoys, training hounds, and a host of other worthwhile things. I believe my friend thought that it was too risky to play a joke on me because of my usefulness in so many of our common pursuits. As I write this I realize he played the ultimate joke on me and Cabell has been dead for nine years.

for Cabell to put his plan into action. In a confidential, almost apologetic, helpful, utterly convincing, and matter-of-fact way that would have fooled the KGB, he leaned over and whispered into the old man's weathered ear. Jerking his thumb to Sluby's vacant seat, he said, "While you were gone that guy took a sip of your beer." Then in an 'I've done my good deed for the day manner', Cabell settled back to see the harvest of the seeds he had so expertly sown.

The old man immediately developed a scowl and frown, clearly visible, although it was superimposed on an already considerable facial topography. About this time Sluby returned with a relaxed expression on his face. The old man fidgeted a little and was obviously in a meditative mood. Then he decided to tell his youthful companion about the foul joke that a mainlander had played on him and what an insult it was to their homeland, that little island in the middle of the Chesapeake about which the universe revolves.

The young tonger took it all in with a gulp of beer, adjusted his hip boots a little, got up, and tapped Sluby on the shoulder. Now, Sluby was no slouch, and he was not easily intimidated. He rose, Cabell rose, I rose and a heated argument began. The young tonger was convinced that his friend had been wronged, and he was determined to right it. I guessed that he was capable of doing so.

At this point Cabell realized the gravity of the situation, quickly paid the bill and tried to get Sluby to leave.

It was then that I remembered my family connections with the home of the tonger and his companion. All I could think of to say as I stepped in front of the tonger was, "My great-grandfather came from Tangier. His name was Captain John Turner. He lived on Nannie's Marsh. Have you ever been there?"

It worked. I was surprised, considering the vicious look in the tonger's eyes. It turned out that he had heard of my great-grandfather from stories told by his grandfather. He became talkative about his life on Tangier, being surprised, even incredulous, that any of us on the mainland knew anything about his little speck in the middle of the Bay and especially the little high marsh area called Nannie's Marsh where my great-grandfather built a home a century ago.

I continued talking to him while Cabell ushered Sluby to the car, which, fortunately, for a change, started without pushing. And with a toot of the horn I bid my colleague adieu and we were all three safe.

Cabell was, as I have said, an expert at starting jokes. His only noticeable shortcoming was that he never developed the knack of terminating them before they got into the domino effect.

UNCLE OBADIAH
WAS A GOOD COUNTER

"Water, water, every where, and all the boards did shrink;
Water, water, every where, nor any drop to drink."
                                        Samuel Taylor Coleridge

Although I was not alive when he was a child, it has always been known that Uncle Obadiah Custis was sort of a black sheep in the family. It seems he was practically useless on the farm. He could not slop the hogs without spilling the slop nor pick up the eggs without dropping them. He never even learned to hook a horse up to a plow. Some say he could have learned these things if he wanted but that he was just purposefully bungling so he wouldn't have to do any chores.

However, he did exceptionally well in school and went right on through the primer without having to repeat a single grade. After this showing, it was decided that he should go for his high school diploma, which he did successfully.

He was good at reading and writing, but his real forte was counting. He could tell how many beans were in a jar or grains of corn on a cob by just looking, and he was never far off. It was once thought that he had inherited all of this smartness from the Custis side of the family. But some doubted this because he was so mild-mannered and easy going and all the Custises were always very hot-tempered and can-tankerous. However, it is likely that not all of these traits were linked up on the same gene, which would explain it.

Uncle Obadiah even went on to college instead of getting himself a good cook stove and a couple of pigs and getting married like normal people did. After college, he got something with a name like 'Highway Scholarship' to go to school in England. I had thought that he was over there studying about roads when I learned about this as a child. As it turned out, however, he eventually became a pharmacist with an extra degree. I suppose this was because he was such a good counter. They say that he could count pills faster than any other druggist on the East Coast, and I believe them.

Uncle Obadiah lived all of his adult life in the city (Philadelphia), but he liked to come back home once in a while, and I must say he never did get uppity like so many local people when they moved away.

He especially liked my friend Cabell because they had grown up together and Cabell had a high school diploma also. Whenever Uncle Obadiah came down for a visit he would always get in on something that Cabell and I were doing. Cabell liked having him around because he was a good subject for a joke, as good as Sluby or Mitt.

Uncle Obadiah usually came down for the Christmas holiday and always would bring to us presents such as ointments, castor oil, Ex-lax, and aspirin. On one of these trips, he motored up to Cabell's house in his twelve-cylinder Packard just as we were loading duck decoys into our truck for a hunt the next day. He asked if he could go. We warned him that it would be cold and we would be gone all day, but he insisted on going, so we included him in our plans.

It was indeed very cold and windy that day on the Chesapeake, but after we got our decoys out we got into the blind and got the stove going; the warmth made us feel like never leaving it again. The problem was that when a duck was shot someone had to go out into the cold to fetch it. The thought of going out almost made us want to miss. But as soon as it was beginning to get light, a flock of southerlies (old squaws) came in, and we shot two of them. No one wanted to go out into the cold to get them in the rough seas, but we all volunteered, which is traditional on the Chesapeake. So just to be fair we all flipped a coin and the odd man was to get the ducks. Uncle Obadiah was the loser, and so he cranked up the outboard and went after the ducks, which had already drifted a long way toward Norfolk in the gale.

While he was out, Cabell and I were sipping hot chocolate in our stocking feet. We both felt thankful for the reprieve but knew that our turn would come. Then Cabell, whose mind was always scheming, came up with a great idea (i.e., if you are not too honest, too ethical, or too religious). His idea was, rather than take turns picking up dead ducks in the rough and cold Chesapeake, that we flip coins every time. Of course, I had to borrow a nickel from Cabell so I could participate. I first figured that this was just a little extra sport with a game of chance, but that was only one part of the two-part plan. The other was that Cabell and I would always show the same side of the coin so that neither of us would ever be the unlucky odd man. That sounded good to me but a little on the evil side considering that Uncle Obadiah was blood kin. However, to make up for it I rationalized that I would go to church on Sunday, the next day, and that would make everything all right. To effect his plan, Cabell suggested that he would scratch his head if we were both to show a head and his tail if we were both to show a tail.

So poor Uncle Obadiah beat his way back against the gale and got back into the blind. He was so cold he could hardly climb out of the boat. Cabell waited a little while for him to thaw out before suggesting that we continue the 'odd man gets the ducks' game. Uncle Obadiah knew that he always had been lucky (that is why he had a Packard), so he readily agreed.

Shortly thereafter a duck came into the decoys, and we shot it. Cabell scratched his head, and we both showed a head on our coin. But Uncle Obadiah had a head also so we did it again. This time Cabell scratched his tail and Uncle Obadiah had a head so he had to go after the duck again. This kept up all morning, and the poor odd man got so cold picking up ducks that he either couldn't or wouldn't shoot anymore.

Uncle Obadiah, who was good at counting, as I have said, estimated that he had travelled over rough seas that day a distance that would have been about the same as if he had gone to Baltimore and back to Tangier Island.

We had a great day shooting ducks from the warmth of the blind, and Uncle Obadiah never caught on. He picked up, by his own count, fifty-two ducks. The only thing he ever said about this evil trick was, "Cabell, you sure do scratch a lot. The next time I come down here I'm going to bring you some lotion that will stop your itching."

A GOOD DAY ON
OCCOHANNOCK CREEK

"You must let them ooze and crawl of their own will on to a knife blade and then lift them gently into your bottle of sea water. And perhaps that might be the way to write this book — to open the page and to let the stories crawl in by themselves."

John Steinbeck

As I have previously told you, Cabell Mapp loved to play pranks. His tricks were not always aimed at humans. Sometimes birds and animals became his targets, like the time we tripped black skimmers with monofilament fishing line. What he considered a real accomplishment was to play a joke on both humans and wild creatures at the same time. Cabell considered certain people prime targets for such amusement; one was Sluby Wallace, another Uncle Obadiah Custis, our duck retriever.

Cabell worked his way up from deck hand to captain of the Chesapeake Bay Ferries which ran from Norfolk to Cape Charles. In fact, he did this three times.

The first time he obtained the rank of Captain he had only worked in that capacity for a year when an aunt died and left him a little money. He quit work right away and spent his time hunting, fishing and spending. When his inheritance ran out, he tried to get his old job back. By then, he had lost his seniority and was required to start over, which probably made him the only deck hand on the Chesapeake with an unlimited-tonnage captain's license.

In a couple of years, he worked his way back up to captaincy. He had been a captain for only a couple of years when he inherited some more money from an uncle and he quit once more. During this second leave of absence he started going fishing every day. He would stay out all day when it wasn't raining or blowing. He became as much of a fixture at the mouth of Occohannock Creek as the Number 10 buoy.

He even got to know the gulls individually. And they obviously knew him and his boat. They would always flock to him as soon as he threw over his anchor. One reason was that he frequently cleaned his fish right where he caught them. I had always told him that gulls could recognize his boat because of the way it was built. Cabell had tried to copy my design, but, when you looked at his boat head on, the stem* had twenty-degree list to starboard. When I pointed this out he insisted he had planned it to allow for the torque of the outboard motor. Anyway, one of the gulls gradually got to be so tame that Cabell could almost touch it if he had food in his hand. This bird was a little bigger, a little dirtier, and a little more aggressive than the average run-of-the-mill gull.

Uncle Obadiah would not go duck hunting with us anymore. However, he did like to fish with Cabell, and one day when he stopped by for a visit and to bring some mustard plaster (poultice) from his Philadelphia drug store we were just getting ready to go roach** fishing. There was a big run at that time and Cabell was delighted to have Uncle Obadiah along. So was I. I knew that even if the fish weren't biting we were certain as the tides to have some fun.

We went to Davis Wharf, where Cabell kept his

---

* The timber at the bow which holds the sides of a boat together.

** Spot - a small, flavorful saltwater fish.

homemade lopsided boat, then motored down Occohannock Creek and anchored close to the Number 10 buoy. There was a deep hole here and a favorite spot for roach.

No sooner had the anchor hit bottom than a flock of gulls flew over to sit expectantly nearby. Among them was Cabell's favorite. We fished for about an hour with nothing but nibbles from pickers*. Cabell and I were getting tired of listening to Uncle Obadiah tell us about the latest pills, purgatives and ointments. When Cabell started talking about the possibility of catching a gull with his bare hands, I knew the time was ripe for a joke.

Cabell believed that a proper joke needed a proper setup or foreplay or else it wouldn't work. He was not interested in jokes obviously precipitated by himself. That was not his style. He disliked pie-in-the-face physical jokes. What he preferred to do, and indeed was expert at, was to allow the jokee (Cabell always being the joker) to entrap himself after a proper setup.

This setup insidiously progressed to the next stage when Cabell reached for the lard tin** which served as his tackle box. He began to change from roach hooks to a smaller type. All the while, he kept talking to Uncle Obadiah about reflexes and how quick he was and how quick a gull was. As he baited up, Cabell casually mentioned that he would bet he could catch a gull with his bare hands. Uncle Obadiah didn't reply but began to take notice when Cabell made a sudden lunge for a gull, just a subtle demonstration of his quickness. Of course, the bird just fluttered away as lightly as a butterfly, settling on the water out of reach. Cabell threw over his line, and no sooner had it touched bottom than he caught two little pickers which he threw back.

* Various small fish not big enough to eat.

** Metal container used for storage of hog fat.

He made another attempt at catching a gull with the same results as the first time. Cabell then got the response he knew would come. Uncle Obadiah said, "I'll bet you ten dollars you can't catch a gull with your hands." Unenthusiastically, Cabell accepted the bet. I knew that mentally he had already added that ten dollars to his purse.

He began to catch little white perch and pinhead croakers, knock them in the head, and throw them to the gulls. He made sure that the big gull got most of the fish. I knew what he was up to and also threw some fish to the gull, hoping that Cabell might give me a dollar from his forthcoming bounty. The more fish the gull ate, the greedier it became and the closer it came to the boat. This is a good example of why greed is one of the ten deadly sins.

Finally, the gull was so overloaded with fish that it didn't have much freeboard left. Cabell slacked up on feeding it. The bird got upset at this neglect and paddled right up to the side of the boat, raving its protest. Cabell had laid his fishing rod down and was waiting for the right moment. He was holding one picker and dropped it right in front of the bird, now beside the boat. When the bird went for the fish, Cabell went for the bird. Both attacks were successful. Uncle Obadiah was surprised and dejected. I'm sure he was determining how many pills he would have to count to make up for the ten dollar loss. Suddenly he brightened up and said, "Cabell, that gull doesn't count because he can't even fly." I thought about this and, according to my interpretation of Chesapeake maritime tradition, I had to admit that there was some merit to his line of reasoning. All the loser needed was the slightest excuse to cry foul, and so he did.

Cabell was already way ahead of Uncle Obadiah, me and the gull. He held the bird for awhile then tossed it into the air. The bird fell to the bottom of the boat. Obadiah had an 'I told you so' expression on his face. Cabell's was full of pseudo-disappointment.

Cabell now prepared for his *coup de théâtre* by holding the big gull up by its hind legs. He jiggled the screaming bird a little and ran his finger into its open maw. Immediately there came forth a deluge of fish like you get when you pull the end rope on a purse seine. Relieved of its burden by about four or five pounds of fish and a lot of slime, the gull easily flew off when Cabell threw it into the air. It flew over to the Number 10 buoy and began to preen, regaining some self-respect after its ordeal.

There was no argument from Uncle Obadiah. He was an honest man. He reached into his pocket and gave Cabell a ten dollar bill.

Then the tide began to run and the roach began to bite. We baited up with the bloodworms we had been saving. Just a small piece of worm about a quarter-inch long is all one needs. We frequently caught roach two at a time. They had the yellow bellies and red eyes that are an indication of being fat and prime.

It was an intellectually and financially successful piscine day.

EXTRACURRICULAR ACTIVITIES

"I had this advantage, at least, in my mode of life, over those who were obliged to look abroad for amusement, to society and the theatre, that my life itself had become my amusement and never ceased to be novel."

Henry David Thoreau

Besides hunting and fishing on the Eastern Shore, there were many other opportunities to enjoy harvesting nature's bountiful gifts.

As you probably know from Biology I, crabs have an exoskeleton and you and I have an endoskeleton. This is the scientific basis for the wonderful sport of mudlarking.

Crabs grow by shedding their hard outer shells, a process called molting. The soft shell underneath is about ten percent larger than the previous hard one, and, in a few hours, it also turns hard. Crabs realize that they will be vulnerable while shedding and waiting to harden. So they pick out a safe, secluded spot in submerged grasses where they can burrow into the mud while waiting to shed and harden. At this stage they are called 'peelers' and are highly sought because they will soon molt and become soft crabs. This is when they are considered a delicacy because you can eat the whole thing. They also are an excellent bait at this stage, probably because they emit a hormone to attract a mate which also attracts predators.

When molting is not imminent they are simply called hard crabs. Then, they are best cooked by steaming. When prepared like this it is best to get your wife or girlfriend to pick the meat out for you.

At certain times of the year, especially during the full moons in May and September, many crabs go through this process at the same time. If in the right spot at low tide, one can find lots of them. They are hard to see, however, because only their eyes are above the surface of the mud. These areas are so muddy that one is lucky to have his own eyes above the mud. A potato sack is the best method of storing the crabs while ploughing through the marsh.

It is worth the trouble when all conditions are right and everywhere one looks a pair of eyes is seen sticking out of the mud. At ten cents per crab, it gives you a great feeling, probably the same feeling, lacking the satisfaction of living close to and off of Mother Earth, that people get when the stock market soars, or when they buy a family farm cheap, from some poor old farmer who has had bad luck, and divide it into little lots and make a fortune. So when you visit us, if all the opera tickets are sold and you don't like polo, we'll take you mudlarking.

At the same time peelers are found in the mud on the seaside, soft crabs can be caught in the Bayside inlets. This is done while standing on the bow of a small boat, pushing along in the shallow water with the handle of a crab net, looking down into the grass. You can also just walk in the shallow water. My mother was an expert at this. She would push her net through the grass just off the bottom and let the crabs fall in. She once told me that her mother would have her, as a child, catch crabs for the entire family of nine when they did not have anything else to eat. One day she caught ninety-four soft crabs right in front of their home on Craddock Creek.

Many times 'doublers' are caught this way. A doubler is a male (jimmy) crab clutching a female peeler or freshly shed soft crab under him. The male can tell a female peeler by its hormones. He will catch her and retain her under his belly, waiting for her to shed. When she does, he will mate with her while she is soft. You can see nature's logic in this.

The doublers are slow and vulnerable because of their female burden. Single soft crabs are also slow because of their temporary flexibility. Usually the lone soft crabs are males, but some are females that didn't get in on the mating.

Of course, you can also dip up hard crabs at the same time; these are not fried as the soft crabs are, but steamed and the succulent meat picked out. There are many other ways of catching crabs, including chicken-necking (a sure sign of a come-here), and traps or pots.

As children, we didn't have any nets, so we would just sneak up on crabs quietly and hold them pinned to the bottom with a stick until the resulting muddy water cleared. We then carefully grabbed them by the back fin to avoid a nasty pinch and stored them in a bucket or basket.

Crabbing was legal, but gull-egging was not. Nevertheless, many people indulged in this oldest of hunting-gathering modes of survival, and I don't know of anyone who ever got caught. I even recall one trip when the Virginia Game and Fish Commission boat took us to the egging grounds. The best places were on the Barrier Islands' beaches and dunes, and the sport started in the spring.

Before gathering eggs to eat, a trip was necessary to remove all the early eggs from the nest. This was because no one but the gull knew when the egg had been laid. It can ruin your breakfast, if not your whole day, if you crack open an egg and a young gull or embryo falls into your spider.

After the nests were cleaned out, the gull-egger came back in a few days and brought buckets or baskets to fill with guaranteed fresh eggs. The eggs were well camouflaged with speckles over a sandy background. One had to be careful not to step on them. In an hour a ten-quart bucket could be filled with these delicious eggs. Their yolks were a very rich orange color like brown hen eggs and, of course, also like brown eggs, were a great aphrodisiac.

Terns laid their eggs at the same time, and these were also eaten. We called the terns 'strikers' because they would vigorously defend their nests by continuously diving at you. Both the males and females took part in this resistance.

We would gather eggs every few days for a couple of weeks because the birds kept on laying new ones as long as you picked them up. After awhile we would stop stimulating the gulls and let them hatch a clutch. We were way ahead of our time as conservationists but never sought any recognition.

In winter, we sometimes went eel-gigging. January or February was a good time. The cold water was crystal clear, and we could see the bottom easily from a small boat. When eels hibernate during the cold months, they make two holes in the mud about a foot or so apart. They do this in the muddy area at the heads of creeks. If you take the eel gig, which is a series of broad blades with barbs arranged in a fan-like manner, jab it into the mud crosswise between the holes, and pull it up quickly, you are apt to come up with an impaled eel. You can catch a potato-basket full if you hit the right spot. Cleaning a basket of eels is no fun. They are so slimy and slippery that you have to throw sand on them to grasp them. Rightfully, it is a traditional chore for your wife or girlfriend.

Also in the winter the mannose or soft-shelled clam can be found from the one-hole sign it leaves in the hard bottom shoreline below the high tide line of the Chesapeake. The hole is this bivalve's communication with the water above it. It is through this hole that the mannose, being completely invisible, protrudes and withdraws its snout for feeding purposes. They sign best on a really cold day and a spade is used to dig them out. They can be buried from twelve to eighteen inches deep. After being caught, they should be placed in water in the icebox where they will obligingly discharge all the sand in their snout, the part you eat.

I have elsewhere described raking clams, but they can also be signed at certain times of the year, usually spring and fall, when the temperature and other conditions are just right. These clams are very hard and live in the mud or sand close to the surface when they can be raked rather than laboriously dug the way one gets mannose.

Clams make several signs. The keyhole sign is a hole in the mud or sand left when the clam retracts its snout. This snout is used for feeding and excretion just like the mannose but it is much shorter. Clam excrement looks like grains of rice, and when a few of them are seen, with or without the keyhole, a clam is found. This is called a litter sign. A clam pick, which is a two-foot long wooden handle with two three-inch teeth, is used to scratch out the clams.

There are many other things one can do to locally enjoy nature, such as picking blackberries or blueberries, gathering wild asparagus or picking up oysters. But I have tried to cover those which contain some element of the chase and are to a certain degree challenging.

BIRD NOTES

"There are millions of people in the world, each of whom keeps at least one active room in the corner of the mind where images of birds abound..."

Michael Harwood

      I do not have a story to tell about birds like <u>That Quail Robert</u>, nor do I have a scientific treatise like Coue's <u>Key To North American Birds</u>. What I do have is some miscellany and recollections of what I thought were interesting avian anecdotes, so I will present them.

      When my oldest son, Bill, was a youngster, he witnessed a pigeon hawk chasing a yellow-billed cuckoo. The cuckoo, in her haste to escape, flew into a window, perhaps mistaking it for a passage to safety, and stunned herself. She fell to the ground and her pursuer flew off. Bill went to the aid of the fallen bird and picked it up. While he was holding it in his hand, it laid an egg, then recovered and flew off. Clearly this was a miscarriage directly related to trauma.

In a barn on our oceanside farm there are many barn swallow nests. I prop the doors open each spring to allow them free access. I keep a close watch on them because once I came upon a snake that had robbed a nest. You could easily see four distended lumps in its stomach or gut, wherever one stops and the other starts in this type of beast. One day I discovered a clutch of eggs in a nest in which there were also four young birds almost ready to fly. There was no way that the parents, young and eggs could fit into the nest all at once, so it appeared that the fledglings were incubating the eggs. I could not tell if the layer of the recent eggs was the parent of the fledglings or not, but I do know the eggs eventually hatched and the birds flew away.

My son, Dave, once picked up a female English sparrow nestling which fell from a nest behind the shutter on the second floor of our home. He found it just as it was about to be caught by a neighbor's cat. David raised the bird by hand. It shared his dorm room during his senior year at William and Mary.

After completing his education, he turned the bird over to my wife and me. It was at first placed in a cage and allowed out at times. It stayed out more and more frequently until the cage was abandoned. At nights, it would roost in a vase that Dave had thrown on a potter's wheel. The bird stuffed this with scraps of paper and cloth. It would not exceed the confines of the kitchen plus an adjoining room. The bird had established its own limits and never made any attempt to cross this invisible, self-imposed boundary.

Tweety, the unusual name we selected for this unusual pet, quickly became a part of the household. She, as it turned out, had some interesting habits, possibly not peculiar to her. One thing that was a daily ritual was a dust bath on top of one's head. There wasn't much dust or dandruff in my head, but apparently the feeling of hair for Tweety initiated a performance exactly like birds go through in dusting themselves. And if you put your hand in the way before she were finished, you would get a nasty peck.

Her diet was exactly the same as ours, and she regularly ate from our plates. Early on, Tweety noticed that I was a sloppy eater, and she would align herself on the floor by my chair and below my right hand, knowing that food would certainly fall from my fork. For some mystifying ornithological reason, she preferred to take her breakfast this way and dine on the table at other meals.

Tweety lived with us for about six years, a very old age for a sparrow. It was a great tragedy for us when one day she died in the space of seconds; one instant chirping and happy, the next, dead. I hope that I am so lucky.

In Tweety's time, English sparrows were a nuisance. However, something happened; I do not know whether it was an epidemic of diseases or from chemicals, but nearly all the sparrows disappeared. That was fifteen years ago and still they are rare. We now pay no attention to the abundant bluebirds but longingly look for the rare English sparrow.

BANTAMS

Some of my first pets were Bantams. They seemed to be of a different nature from other chickens, more friendly, especially. Bantam hens make great foster parents. I think they would hatch alligator eggs and raise the offspring if they were given the chance.

I once put two Canada geese eggs under a broody (ready to set) Bantam. She turned the eggs dutifully over, though they were three or four times as large as her own. She hatched them with great patience, even though they have to be incubated a little longer than chicken eggs that hatch in twenty-eight days.

After hatching, things went along normally for a few days. The hen thought the goslings were her own natural children and they thought she was their mother or whatever geese think along those lines. Before long, however, the goslings, in their ever-increasing wanderings, discovered a pond close to the barn where they were hatched. They had probably wondered why their feet were webbed and their mother's were not. They may never have figured this out, but they were quick to learn to swim.

The goslings entered the water at every opportunity. This created a problem for the bantam hen that was by nature a good mother. She would stand on the edge of the pond, quite flustered, frustratingly clucking and trying to entice her errant foster children back to dry land. No matter how long they stayed in the water she never abandoned them for a moment and was always at the pond's edge when they came out.

There was another crisis every evening when it came time to roost. Geese sleep by necessity and instinct on the ground when they are young and later, on the water. All chickens roost off the ground, which gives them some measure of protection from land predators. Every evening I herded the trio into a safe enclosure and every evening one could witness a conflict of the primordial survival and maternal instincts in the dedicated foster mother. She would always, as light faded, take a position on a roosting bar a few feet off the floor of the enclosure. From here she would plead with her children to join her. After a frustrating few minutes she would descend to the floor and cover one with each wing to protect and warm them overnight.

As they grew, brooding these geese became increasingly difficult. When they were each several times her diminutive size, she still tried to cover them with her wings at night. It was a pathetically comical sight to witness her with wings almost straight up in the air in a vain attempt to brood her giant children.

<u>OSPREY</u>

The bird of prey most conspicuous in our area is the osprey; it isn't necessary to be near water to see them. Arriving in mid-March, they spend a lot of their time over land, looking for limbs and grass for nests which they begin to build anew or refurbish immediately upon arrival. The osprey can, of course, pick up dead branches from the ground, but it actually prefers to snap them off a tree by grabbing them in flight. They come at it in an unhesitating and unintimidated way, grabbing what they think is a breakable branch as if it were a fish. I have watched this maneuver often, hoping to see a branch that didn't snap off. But they must be good judges of the strength of the wood because it never fails to snap.

In times past, many people shot all hawks on sight. That included the beautiful osprey, usually murdered under the pretense that they eat fish or that their nests will kill a good tree. Each excuse is ridiculous. Most identifications of this bird's catch have shown menhaden, eel, hogchoke*, or other fish of no commercial or sporting value. Even if they dined on nothing but the best fish, the impact on the population would be minimal. I would rather see an osprey catch a big trout than eat a trout myself any day.

There was a time when the Coast Guard destroyed all nests, eggs, and young birds when the osprey made its home on a buoy or day-marker. No longer is this allowed and with the abandonment of certain poisons, such as DDT, there are now excellent numbers of these magnificent birds around.

I have heard or read (anyhow, it came to me by supposed authority) that at times an osprey sinks its claws into a fish too big to take aloft and, since the claws cannot unlock instantly, it drowns. I have never witnessed this, but once I did witness something similar.

When I was a young boy, I was riding around the back roads with an older crony looking for something related to nature; I've forgotten what. He saw an osprey sitting on the limb of a tree clutching a freshly caught fish in its talons. The bird was beautiful as it sat in the top of the old pine, its wings balancing against the wind.

My friend stopped the truck, took out his shotgun and fired at the 'fish hawk'. The poor creature did not flinch or fly. But you could see the life begin to leave its beautiful body. Very slowly it rotated forward and down around the limb, which it continued to clutch along with its fish. It did not scream or flap its wings or offer any protest to its senseless death. It continued this rotation until it hung, head and wings straight down to the floor of the woods fifty feet below. It held this pathetic position for a considerable time, obviously dead or nearly so, yet its needle-sharp talons still locked onto the branch on which it had a few minutes before rested in peace with its morning catch. Finally, the talons lost their

* A small species of flounder.

grip and the noble bird fell to the forest floor.

We went over to look at it; its brilliant yellow eyes were half-closed and blood trickled from its mouth. The speckled trout was still flopping and still held by the bird's sharp talons; ironically it had outlived its captor. It was a temptation to take the fish, but neither of us made a move to steal it from its legitimate though now deceased owner. We had no more right to the fish than we did to the bird's life. It was a senseless killing. We left both there on the pine shatters beneath the huge tree.

The death of this bird was so quiet and dignified that it affected me (to the extent that I write of it a half-century later), and more importantly, I think it affected my partner, the culprit. I suspect this because as the bird clung to the branch he said to me, "They kill the trees with their nests." It was evident that he really did not care whether that was true or not. He was meekly and halfheartedly trying to convince himself and me that he had done the proper thing. I do not think he ever shot another osprey.

In the intervening half century, I have erected many platforms for osprey nests and splinted several broken wings. However, I will never feel that I have paid my debt for my participation in the death of the splendid bird killed by my friend as I stood by and failed to ask him to stop.

CANADA GEESE

At one time, Canada geese were the biggest game we had on the Eastern Shore. We did not see deer in our area until 1960 or so.

Geese had a special meaning, a special place, and a special mystique about them which eluded other waterfowl. Now be certain that I am not slighting the canvasback or the black duck, or even the little bufflehead, because I was and still am infatuated by all waterfowl. But the Canada had a presence and a place and a personality no other duck or goose could match.

In the fall, as the fires from the hog killings pushed little columns of smoke upwards and the first frost came, the Canada geese made their appearance in long skeins and vees in the autumn sky. Even if you could not see them, you could hear them. One even heard them in the dark hours of night while lying awake in a bed of goose-feather mattresses that were so snug and warm in the winter nights when the wood stove, rooms and floors away, was extinguished until the next morning.

The arrival of the geese signaled a change of seasons in autumn just as the bloom of the shad bush and calls of laughing gulls did in spring. The long skeins of Canada geese and their honking were eagerly awaited. They usually began to appear in October. It was a time to exchange clam rakes, crab nets, and fishing lines for shotguns, decoys, hounds and oysters.

Geese and swans distinguish themselves from their promiscuous brother waterfowl by their devotion to each other and earn for themselves, perhaps because of this trait, a longevity of thirty to forty years. This devotion, while apparent to some extent year-round, is especially obvious during the nesting season, when the gander will unhesitatingly attack anyone approaching his mate. When the young hatch out, both goose and gander become attentive parents. They are, therefore, usually able to raise a higher percentage of their brood than ducks.

There are times when this devotion can get misplaced. I remember one gander that was romantically attached to a cow. Obviously, this bond was of the purest nature, since the potential for physical satisfaction was minimal. Everywhere the cow went, so went the goose; this continued daily for years. It appeared to be a one-sided affair, since the cow never showed the slightest attention to the goose. They say that unrequited love is worse than hell.

In another instance, my friend Bagley Walker had a one-leg Canada goose that became attached to his Labrador retriever. Everywhere the dog went the gander was sure to follow. This goose showed the same signs of protection as his brothers did to natural mates. Each night when the dog went to his kennel, the goose stood guard and would not rest.

DUCKS

Of all the creatures great and small on the earth, I think ducks fascinate me, captivate me and motivate me most. At least they have done so at one time or another, more than any other form of life. All children are interested early on in animals, probably because they move and they are different. It does not matter if the child is of metropolitan or rural origin. The interest is naturally there. On this innocent interest of childhood, empires are built, books are written and movies are made. Now the great recreation parks and the television networks capitalize on this trait, which may be properly called an instinct.

My first encounter with a wild duck came when I was spending some time with my Aunt Dorothy and Uncle Melvin on Craddock Creek, about one-half mile from the Chesapeake Bay. One of my older cousins, Wilson Custis, had been hunting and proudly brought back a drake bufflehead, locally known as a butterball. He left it lying on a bench in the porch. I would guess he had sneaked up on it and shot it from the shoreline as it was swimming. It was a thrill to see, touch and smell this beautiful duck with its striking black and white markings, pink feet and blue bill. This bird made an indelible impression on me. I think this was the first time I thought about going hunting for ducks.

It was not long after this that another cousin, Vernon, brought home a pair of black mallards he had shot in a pond close to a nearby creek. He had used an old farm truck for this outing, and he was proud as he drove into the yard with these large dark brown-colored birds, which were a welcome addition to the table.

A few years later, I was allowed to have a gun and began to carve duck decoys and prowl the shorelines, hoping to get within range of an unsuspecting duck.

As some children grow, this interest disappears and, with some, the interest grows with the child. I suspect that more rural children than metropolitan children retain this interest.

Now let's get back to ducks. I think I always have envied them. They can dive, swim, fly, float and walk. They come in many varieties, an array of sizes, colors, shapes and habits that cannot fail to attract attention and admiration from anyone. Remember, I am writing about wild ducks (not tame varieties, although I had a tame duck as one of my first pets.)

The Eastern Shore of Virginia was obviously shaped and molded by some duck god, as one can see from a map. With the Chesapeake Bay on the west and the ocean on the east, it is a narrow peninsula that is almost eaten away by inlets, bays and marshes and offers some of the best waterfowl habitat in the United States. A few generations ago, the area was famous for its market hunting. Canvasbacks and other ducks were trapped and shot and shipped to Baltimore, Philadelphia and New York by the barrel. This illegal and commercial hunting is a subject which could fill a large book. It was carried on by locals in a variety of ways, all of them outlawed when regulations became necessary in the early part of this century.

Live decoys, baiting, trapping, punt shooting, and various combinations of these, before, during, and after the season, night or day, decimated the ducks. These practices, which continue today, combined with encroachments on nesting areas and mismanagement, will insure that we will never again see the great flocks of waterfowl I was fortunate enough to briefly glimpse.

I must admit that in my youth I was guilty of some of the illegal practices mentioned above, especially baiting with corn. My cousin, Melvin, and I for years baited a small pond deep in a woods (which we now own). We would never shoot birds on the water or shoot into large flocks, and we never sold our bag. But some of the things we did were illegal. We shot ducks until we figured we couldn't carry any more, and that was our limit. All were eaten; there was no waste.

More Chickens

When I stayed with Melvin during summers, we had great sport with chickens. Every spring a batch of biddies was purchased by mail order. After being kept in a brooder until they feathered out, they were released and ran around the yard and nearby fields during the day.

We were told to keep them out of the garden in a gentle manner, and we did; keep them out of the garden, that is. Since we each had BB guns, this was our method of choice, gentle or not. Every time we saw a chicken encroach upon the forbidden garden we took out after it, shouting and shooting. We only did this when Uncle Melvin was out of sight; otherwise we just coaxed them out so they hardly knew what was going on.

Although we figured that sooner or later statistics would probably catch up with us, we were having a great time firing our guns at these offending beasts. It was amusing to watch them jump in the air and run off after being stung by a pellet.

One Sunday, while we were having our usual fried-chicken dinner, Uncle Melvin suddenly stopped chewing on a golden-fried back, done to perfection as only my Aunt Dorothy could do it. He paused in his repast and did a little extra maneuvering with his jaw, cheek and tongue, then held his hand to his mouth and spat out a BB. He looked at it, then he looked at us. He threw the pellet on the table and didn't say a word. He just looked, but we got the message clearly; we would be spanked if he ever bit into another BB lead shot.

I don't think I enjoyed another fried chicken dinner that summer. After all, we had fired several hundred rounds, and quite likely there was another chicken running around or perhaps already in the pot with a pellet just under its skin, waiting to be bitten by Uncle Melvin.

One of our favorite pastimes was catching a chicken and laying it on its back to hypnotize it. While holding it down, we would make several circles in the dirt with a stick around its head. After doing this and gently releasing the bird, it would remain hypnotized and motionless for several minutes. Once we had twelve fryers all lined up on the ground before any of them started getting up and running off. We firmly believe this to be a world record. To achieve this there had to be the proper combination of many factors. First, you had to be quick and adept at grabbing a chicken on the run by its feet or any other appendage that presented itself. More important was timing. The more circles you did around the chicken's head the longer it stayed hypnotized. However, there was a point of diminishing returns when the earlier hypnotized birds started to get up and run away. We practiced and experimented, but twelve was the best we could do. That was a sultry day in August of 1941.

Chickens were different and better for eating in the old days. To begin with, they looked better; the black and white finely striped Plymouth Rock was much prettier and more interesting than the paltry white food-conversion machines of today. The eggs were a deep brown with a rich orange yolk that very seldom contained an embryo when it was cracked into a spider, but you don't see the Plymouth Rock anymore; I suspect they are now outnumbered by condors.

The biggest difference was in the taste. They were fat and golden, quite unlike today's bleached and blued store-bought product. I think a lot of it has to do with diet. They ran free until caught for the pot and there was a wide range of food available, including the shelled corn we sprinkled before them each day. They also ate bugs, caterpillars and fish heads. I vividly recall watching one old rooster eat the maggots out of a dead rat. If he ended up in the pot, I prayed that when he was penned and purged he would get an extra day or two of this routine death-row treatment.

I loved fried chicken dearly but did not like the violence associated with the birds' death for the pot. After being pent up in a purge coop for a few days with no horse excrement or maggots, only golden corn kernels to eat, they were executed in one of two ways. One way was to grasp a bird's hind legs and lay its head on a block of wood from the ever-present woodpile and decapitate it with an axe. Another way was just to grasp it by the head and whirl it through the air with a twisting motion which broke the neck. This was preferred by many farm women because it was less bloody. Old Aunt Mattie had this latter method down to a science and could gracefully do two at a time, one clockwise and one counterclockwise, reminding me of a juggler or baton twirler. I do not know which treatment the chickens preferred, but the clean cut of the axe and block of wood appealed to me. I suppose the chickens really didn't care. As Nehru said when asked if he preferred the Allies or the Axis, that was "like asking a chicken if it wanted to be fried in grease or butter".

CROWS

No writing about birds would be complete without mentioning crows. In our area, we have two varieties, the common crow and the fish crow. The latter is smaller, less numerous and has a distinctly different call.

As a youngster, I loved to hunt crows by calling them with a factory-made call. Later, I learned to do this using just my voice. It was a lot of fun in the spring when the young birds had just learned to fly and had not yet learned to be wary. As kids, we shot lots of them, usually early in the morning and in the evening. We learned that migrant laborers working local farm crops loved to eat them, and we always took them to the camps where these unfortunate field workers lived. I, too, have eaten much crow in my lifetime.

Crows of all ages are smart birds. In support of this, I'd like you to try to remember if you ever saw a crow road-kill. I have seen owls, hawks, buzzards, ducks, geese and practically every bird in our community lying dead on the highway and back roads, but never a crow. When you consider that they spend a considerable portion of their life scavenging road-kills and garbage thrown from motor vehicles, this speaks well of their intelligence.

I once had three pet crows which Cabell Mapp and I captured. Their names were Tom, Dick and Harry. As they learned to fly, they would make a small circular flight and return to my shoulder. Over time, they flew farther and farther and then began to pitch on neighbors' houses instead of returning to me, and I would have to go fetch them. Finally, they were released in a nearby woods, and I don't think that I ever saw them again, but, of course, all crows look alike.

DOGS I HAVE KNOWN

"Though prejudice perhaps my mind befogs,
I think I know no finer things than dogs."
                              Hally Carrington Brent

It is common practice to compare dogs to humans and make the dog come out on top. The object is to satisfy the demands of the distraught human, wronged by his fellows and wishing to allow his soured mind to bathe in the healing thought: most humans are S.O.B.'s, but most dogs are nice.

Many like to compare the attributes of dogs with the attributes of humans. This is not only fun; it also has considerable merit.

My experience with each species does not observe the emergence of either as a model of character compared to the other. To put it in a nutshell, which is always a convenient place to put such unfathomable musings, I have found that a fair portion of humans are no good as well as a fair portion of dogs. And this is not to say that I am a real shoo-in into the elite by any means of judgment.

What I have found, and this is a definite scientific genetic fact, is that in pedigreed dogs and self-styled pedigreed humans there are definitely traits either inherited or forced upon them by the environment which make them fall into the questionable category. Now I will give you enough examples of my reasoning to make you want to hide your coat of arms.

I have already told you about Spot, my first dog. I really don't remember him well, and honestly I am not sure that he was actually a he. On looking back, however, I feel for sure that he was not a purebred, and undoubtedly he was a gift from someone. I do remember that he liked me and I liked him and I missed him tremendously after he was gone.

Later on my sister Nancy and I had a pseudo-collie. This dog could tell time to within five minutes without a watch. He loved to meet the school buses, and I know that he was always a few minutes early every day for years to greet all the children getting off at the crossroads of Belle Haven, the local stop. (In the those days there was one stop and everyone in town got off or on there. Now these stops are every few feet in front of every yard. If you are ever in a hurry behind one of these creeping buses you will get awfully impatient while you wait for each mother, usually in curlers and a nightgown, to wipe the egg and cereal from her child's mouth while the bus driver patiently waits for his rider before moving to the next homestead one-hundred feet down the line.)

Anyway, his name was Rusty and he was a good dog, but one day he didn't meet the bus and never met another. I always suspected that he ended up in a medical experiment somewhere, especially after I took a physiology course at the Medical College of Virginia.

Elsewhere I have told you about my unsatisfactory experience with a Chesapeake retriever in Alaska. But I have had other experiences right here on the Eastern Shore with other pure-bred retrievers, namely the Labrador.

I had heard so much about what wonderful creatures these dogs were I decided that I would save some money for one with papers and really have a nice companion for my life in the field. The dog I purchased was solid black. This was in the days before they started having the chocolate then the yellow variety. It seems that they are getting lighter all the time, and I suspect that they want to get all the black out of them and end up with all white Nordic-type labs.

My dog was nice in the beginning, but as he grew from puppyhood he began to chase my chickens and ducks, so I tried to train him not to do that. I knew for certain that he was trainable and intelligent because he had a pedigree.

I came home one day to discover that he had killed several of my best-laying hens. I was a little ruffled by this and decided to try an old-time guaranteed remedy, which was to grasp a dead chicken by its feet and use it as a weapon to beat the criminal dog. This I did so severely that my old faithful dog Nellie, who was present as I punished the Labrador, bit me. For good measure I added another sure-fire remedy to this punishment. Actually, either of these, according to old-timers, was sufficient, but I suspected that I had a problem on my hands so I decided to administer both sure-fire remedies at once.

The second remedy was to wire the chicken or duck or calf or whatever the canine had killed to his collar and let it rot, assuming that in the final analysis the dog would be so sick of the close proximity of his decaying and clinging victim that he would never hurt another.

So after the brutal beating with the chicken I took a piece of bailing wire and secured the feet of the bird to the dog's collar and picked them up and threw both into a pen. At this point the dog was only slightly ahead of the chicken in life, but I knew for certain that this combination treatment would cure him and we would be boon companions for life.

I went to bury the other chickens in my garden on the theory that there is some good in everything. After this salvage job I went to give my dog some water and see if he were still alive. If he were, I fully expected that he would be cowering in a corner.

When I opened the door to the pen he met me with a wagging tail which I suppose in itself is a testament to his stupidity, but he was alone. The chicken was gone and I at first thought that the collar must have come loose. I saw, however, that the chicken feet were still tightly wired to the intact collar and nowhere in the pen were there any remains of my laying hen. The exact whereabouts of the chicken was apparent from the distended belly of my pedigreed dog.

A few days later, I let my dog out of the pen and the first thing he did was eat the cork handle off my favorite fishing rod. I gave him to someone I didn't especially like.

On the flip side, I will tell you about my favorite dog, Folly, who still lives as I write this but probably will not make it until you read it.

When my oldest son, Bill, was in college he answered an ad in a newspaper and paid ten dollars for a black and white puppy that had some of the characteristics of a collie-like sheep dog. They said he was a border collie. About this time, another son, Dave, picked up a nondescript dog named Buddy from the local S.P.C.A., and the two dogs grew up together. Early on, Folly showed his extremely jealous nature and wouldn't let Buddy give us any attention. In a few years the gentle Buddy suddenly died. Folly lived on though, and he and I grew to be very close. He loved boats and cars and would not miss an excursion out on the water in any kind of weather.

Folly was very protective of his territory, and one day I saw him viciously attack and drive away two huge wire-haired terriers, dogs so prized for their fighting abilities that mountain lion hunters out West always include one in their pack of hounds, even though they don't bay or trail. The terriers are there for their fighting ability, which keeps the hounds safe from the lions. Anyway, these two huge terriers left our area in a hurry. Of course, this is not exactly a fair evaluation of the wire-haired terrier breed for two reasons. One, they belonged to a recently retired come-here couple from up north, and chances are their lion-fighting experience was limited. Also, Folly had the home field advantage, always important, at least from a psychological view.

Folly is the only dog I have ever had that would actually engage in a game with me. Liking tennis but not having many friends to play with made it difficult to practice. However, when I practiced serves, Folly would retrieve the balls, but his retrieving was a little different from that of any other dog I have ever known. After bringing the ball back, he would stop a few feet from me and with a sideways thrust of his head he would throw the ball so that it would bounce. He knew that the bounce was important, and I think he learned this from television.

Elsewhere in this book you will read about Mitt's bear dog which conquered its humble origins and became a great hound out West. Sometimes humans, like dogs, also rise above their supposed genetic limitations.

I have met many dogs and many S.O.B.'s in my lifetime, and I cannot close this chapter without mentioning a humble dog that stayed humble and whose lovable nature earned him a place in my memory.

One of the favorite places for local people of a certain mentality to dump their garbage is close to a branch* along side a back road. I suppose the slight dip in topography affords these thoughtless people a little secrecy when they part with their trash. It was along one of these branches, beside a public back road, that I first encountered a dog my boys named Dump.

At the same time I first saw this bedraggled bit of

_____
* A small, fresh-water stream.

caninity, he saw me approaching in my car and respectfully stood up beside some garbage and wagged his tail. I rode on by.

The next day, going in the opposite direction, I approached the area and the dog was still there. As I drove past, he again rose and wagged his tail. This time, I looked in the rear view mirror and when I was about a light pole away he stopped wagging his tail and settled down again beside the garbage which was beside the road, beside the branch.

That afternoon on my way home, I again traveled the same route and nothing was changed except a few more bags of garbage appeared to have been dumped. The dog, on seeing me approach, again rose from the same spot and wagged his tail. The difference was that this time I could not pass him by. I stopped my car and went over to him. The closer I got, the faster his tail wagged. I touched him and asked him to come with me. He did.

Closer inspection revealed that he was average size and a dingy dark average color. In short, he was probably about the most unremarkable dog in the way of physique that I have ever seen. He was the final, ultimate result of mixed breeds mixing with mixed breeds for so many generations that he was actually a perfect example of a standard, average, median, composite, run-of-the-mill dog. His only remarkable attributes were his smell and his personality. The former could be changed; the latter needed no adjustment.

My three sons were enthusiastic about my lucky find and, after I related the circumstances of his discovery, they promptly and affectionately named him Dump.

Dump was not with us long, his prior maltreatment and neglect, symbolized by his being left in a branch, had affected his health and after a few months he died, still wagging his tail. We buried him on a high spot near our cabin at the head of Occohannock Creek.

He did not do tricks, he did not chase rabbits or bears, he did not bark at burglars or nip at strangers, but, like Will Rogers, "he never met a man that he didn't like". He did not have a pedigree but he *was* noble.

HALF-MILE RELAY

*"We had nothing to do but run. We couldn't afford any kind of equipment,
so we ran and ran and ran."*

Jesse Owens

There were times, when I was not too busy hunting
and fishing, that I went to school and I did enjoy, if not excel
at, sports. In 1951 high school football, our record was 6-0
and we figured that we would go undefeated for the nine-game
season, but that was not to be.

My cousin, Melvin, who was very quick, was our star
halfback. During the early minutes of our seventh game, his
leg was hurt, forcing him to run with a severe limp which
slowed him down to the extent that some of the faster
opposition could catch him, and when the other team had the
ball, they could sometimes get away from him. This team
finally scored on us. Although we did not know it at the time,
it was the beginning of the end.

Finally, with just a couple of minutes left, Melvin
broke away and limped eighty yards to the two-yard line.
That was as close as we got. We lost, 7-0. We went on to
lose the next two games also, to teams we had soundly beaten
earlier in the season.

The next spring Melvin and I went out for the half-mile relay team. Although he still had a limp from his football injury, Melvin made it with ease, along with our fellow students, Herman Atkinson and Tommy Parks. I also made the team.

Melvin was the fastest and was the anchor man and Tommy had the quickest reaction and was the starter. I was second and Herman was third.

We practiced for the local meet held each May on the horse racing track at Keller Fair Grounds. The event was called *Field Day*, and all the local high schools turned out and competed in many events. That is, all except the black high schools, which was just as well for none of us would have won anything.

Our relay team easily won the half-mile event (two hundred twenty yards per person) and Melvin limped in about sixty yards ahead of the second-place finisher. This victory entitled us to travel to Charlottesville to participate in the state track meet.

This was a major outing for us because we had never been to the mountainous western part of our state. The biggest hill we had ever seen was a manure pile. When the appointed time came, our high school principal, Leonard Johnson, proudly loaded us into his old Plymouth and we headed west on a nine-hour trip to the University of Virginia.

After we had passed Richmond and were about half-way to Charlottesville, we noticed what we thought were dark, low-lying clouds in the distance. As we motored on, we soon perceived (being astute observers) that they were not clouds but trees and land, way up in the air. We had seen our first hills.

We spent the night in a college dorm and the next day went out to the athletic field. We could see immediately that horses did not run on it, and instead of dirt the track was gravel. This aroused our curiosity but did not bother us because our feet were tough from going barefooted all the time anyway. What did bother us were the fancy track suits of the other schools from across the state. These athletes were sporting colorful matching tops and bottoms and they all had track shoes. We were unshod. Each of us wore swimming trunks except Tommy, who had something on that was less water-related. Melvin's trunks had flowers on them, mine had fish, and Herman's had birds. They were all pretty enough but somehow just didn't fit in with all those athletic uniforms which were sure to make a person much more fleet of foot.

We anticipated nothing but humiliation and shame when we took our places, but at the starter's gun, Tommy jumped ahead of our rivals and gave me the baton twenty yards ahead of anyone else. I managed to add a little more distance to it when I gave it to Herman, and likewise he added some more distance to it. Things were looking good when Herman entered the baton-passing area. This is where things began to go wrong. In trying to pass the baton, either Herman or Melvin dropped it. In the time it took Melvin to pick it up we were suddenly not forty yards ahead, which is a huge lead in a seventy-five percent complete half-mile relay, but twenty-five yards behind, an even larger deficit when there is only two hundred twenty yards left in the race. Since Melvin, our anchor man, was still very fast, he began to limp up behind the huge guy now in the lead. In the last fifty yards, Melvin began to limp on by this giant whose strides were a third again as long as his. Just a few yards before the finish, Melvin was obviously going to pass the leader. It looked as if glory was ours, as flowered bathing trunks passed numbered athletic shorts. In an instant, however, Melvin was flying headlong through the air. He had been tripped by his competitor. In that split second the race was lost by inches. Melvin slid across the finish line in second place.

The winner set a new state record.

THE MARSH

"Out walking in the frozen swamp one grey day,
I paused and said, 'I will turn back from here.
No, I will go on farther — and we shall see.'
The hard snow held me, save where now and then
One foot went through. . ."

                                    Robert Frost

In my youth, I spent much time on my Uncle Melvin and Aunt Dorothy Drummond's farm on Craddock Creek close to the Chesapeake. From my cousins, uncle, and other farmers, I often overheard conversation about a place called *The Marsh*. The more I heard the more my curiosity and imagination grew. I think my mind's view of this place was probably similar to a modern child's perception of outer space. It seemed so far away, so wild, so wonderful, and so dangerous.

I cannot recall exactly when I first heard of The Marsh but I have no doubt that it was during one of my visits, sometimes for as long as a year or more, to my Uncle Melvin's and Aunt Dorothy's. As you can see from the map on page *xii*, they lived not far from this wilderness' southern border. I remember clearly one Halloween an old lady telling stories about the *Yahoo*, a strange creature often heard but never seen that lived on The Marsh. I'll tell you more about this later.

One day, my older cousin, Vernon, came back from

The Marsh with a trio of beautiful red-legged black ducks he had shot. He was very proud of them and described his long trek through the marsh mud. My Uncle Melvin frequently mentioned his 'coon hunting on The Marsh. So, insidiously as a lifting fog, I became aware of this vast, enchanted, dangerous, faraway place. I knew I would someday roam over it.

As my cousin Melvin and I grew and expanded our bounds, The Marsh was the first place we began to probe. We had saved our money from picking strawberries, tomatoes, and other crops and had ordered our first shotguns from Montgomery Ward. With guns on our shoulders we claimed to be hunters, and we knew from rumor that The Marsh was a hunter's paradise, especially for waterfowl. We began our assault in the fall and every Saturday approached The Marsh from a different direction, penetrating a little farther each time.

On one of our first forays, we decided to approach along the sandy shores of the south side of Nandua Creek, the northern boundary of Melson's Marsh. We were confident of making some inroads on the place. At the same time, we felt a bit anxious about getting lost or stuck in the mud or eaten by the Yahoo. As we walked along on a very quiet sunny morning, our guns on our shoulders, we heard a strange whistling sound on the other side of the trees, a sound just like the bombs we had heard at the Saturday- night movies. It was very quickly approaching us, and we did not know what it was or what to do. Suddenly we threw ourselves down on the sand, expecting to be hit by a bomb, falling star or something from outer space. As we hit the sand, we looked up to see what was on the brink of destroying us. At first we perceived it to be about twenty separate missiles; then we saw that these missiles had a pair of wings each. We then recognized a flock of ducks and from later experience we learned that they were goldeneyes, locally know as whistlers from the whistling sound of their wings. Lots of birds make a similar sound in flight. Others, such as the owl, make none. But none comes even close to the whistlers.

I have often wondered about the purpose of this noise. Perhaps it allows these beautiful diving ducks to stay together in their flights over deep and foggy waters.*

Now that I have confessed to you our naivete, let me offer an excuse for our embarrassing reaction to this innocent flight of whistlers.

During the war from which our country had just emerged, the Chesapeake Bay was an important maritime practice area for bombs and shells. Frequently as we worked in the field we could hear stray shells whistling through the air. One morning, as we walked the two miles or so along a dirt road to a rendezvous with the school bus, we came upon a fresh crater about thirty feet in diameter and eight feet deep, only a few steps off our path. Once, my Uncle Melvin noticed two big holes about five inches in diameter in the metal roof of the stables next to the barn. So we were, if not in a state of shell shock, at least aware of things that could hurt going through the air.

On that day, we did not probe much farther, possibly because our egos as explorers had been tarnished. We had in mind the same tactic used on the Poles, the Northwest Passage and Source of the Nile: probe, accumulate knowledge, and come back and probe farther.

Soon after that we were back on the same trail again. This time we went beyond our old mark and continued through The Marsh until we came to a small body of water. We later learned that it was Mason's Gut. It looked about one cow pasture wide, and on the other side we saw what we thought was a flock of ducks. We hunkered down in the bushes to see if they would swim to our side so they could be slain. There was a fog on the water and visibility was poor,

*See Winslow Homer's painting, *A Right and a Left*

but I, being the ornithologist of the pair, positively identified them as black ducks. This conclusion, which was now fact, made us even more eager because this species was a culinary delight and we wanted to contribute to the family larder.

We waited and waited and after a good while they appeared a little larger, so we assumed that they were getting closer. In view of this progress, we decided to wait some more. The birds seemed to get larger and larger, but something was wrong because now they did not seem to be getting closer. The fog began to lift a little, and our flock of ducks turned into a set of roots from an old pine tree stump. The ebbing of the tide made these roots look like they were getting larger as the water receded around them. That was forty-five years ago, and the old pine roots are still there, and my companion never lets me forget my positive identification of the elusive black ducks whenever we are in this area.

So it went, each foray taking us deeper into The Marsh until finally we conquered it and made a path all the way to the Chesapeake's shore. And this is where the action was.

As you can see from the map on page *xii*, this frontage on the Bay is about three miles, with sand dunes, then there are ponds full of grass and miles of tidal streams on the north end. It is a waterfowler's dream.

Besides the natural ponds bordering the shore there are several small ones more to the interior and surrounded by pine forest. Most are shallow and are frequently dry. One of the deeper ones is known as the *Cowhole*. Supposedly, according to local legend, it was dug by slaves a couple of hundred years ago as a watering place for cattle. Even in my memory, cattle were raised on The Marsh to take advantage of grazing on the salt meadow hay which carpets several hundred acres. The Cowhole does show evidence of digging, but it appears that it probably was a natural pond, enlarged to prevent total drying up during summer months.

I first heard of this magical place in little bits and pieces from my uncles and others, and Melvin and I began to search for it in our explorations. We finally found it by tracing a small drainage area back to the pond itself. I think we discovered it during summer. When the hunting season began, we appeared on its banks often to try to get a black duck or a mallard. It was a grand place for waterfowl from September until March.

In later years, when we became more lethal, we built a small blind in the middle of a clump of saltwater bushes and at the foot of several tall Loblolly pines. We nailed a drift-wood board to the trees, making an ideal blind, completely natural.

The pond was 'L' shaped, and the blind was in the angle portion, so this gave us two major shooting directions, depending on the wind direction, which on the best days was from the northwest. To get to this pond (which was so secluded that the property's owner did not know about its abundance of ducks) was such a hard trek through marsh and underbrush that he let us hunt it almost exclusively for about ten years.

It was indeed difficult to reach this spot, but it was worth the effort. The trip took about thirty minutes of walking through the needlegrass marsh, which could be painful and dangerous to the eyes if you fell. Between the clumps of marsh were myriad potholes, and after a high tide the water might go over our boots if we were not lucky and careful.

Since we felt sorry for the remaining ducks after shooting so many, we always took one hundred pounds of corn with us on each hunting trip or at least twice a week to feed them, whether we shot any or not. We were conservationists well ahead of our time, as I have said before; but the federal people up north had made laws against this practice so in our efforts to help the birds, we had to be careful. To make our hunting appear legal, we always put out a few wooden decoys. However, even without these it would have been impossible to keep the ducks out of the pond.

The ducks were never present when we arrived at the pond, but with the first hint of daylight great flocks of black ducks and mallards would begin to come in. We never shot into these flocks for two reasons. One was that the flash from the gun showed up in the semi-darkness and scared the ducks as much as the sound of the gun. The other was that it was not good to scare a whole flock just to kill two or three birds. So we made it a practice to try to scare the birds off for the first half hour or so. Then by the time it was fully light they would come back in twos, threes and smaller flocks. We got some very good shooting this way. We had some self-imposed limits which were as many birds as we could transport out of the place in two potato sacks. As far as I know, we never violated this self-imposed restriction.

When it was very cold and windy it was nice to go to the Cowhole and hunt in the shelter of the woods and not have to battle the bitter waves in our open-water stake blind near the edge of the Chesapeake Bay. However, if conditions were so that the pond was frozen over with the slightest skim of ice, we would get no shooting at all. It always amazed me that the ducks knew when the pond was frozen and never came. They would not even fly over on a surveillance flight to check out the ice conditions. Somehow, they knew this without having to see it, whereas Melvin and I had to make the trip to find out for ourselves; unless, of course, it was so cold that there was no question about it.

Nearly all the ducks we shot were black ducks, mallards, greenwinged teal with a few wood ducks. True, we shot too many, but all were put to good use and never did we allow a bird to be wasted. Many poor families that would otherwise have had lean pickings had duck or goose for Christmas or Thanksgiving.

Of course, in the days of our youth, we knew little about outboard motors, and the only way we could approach the Bay shore ponds was to walk a mile or so past the Cowhole and through the mud and needlegrass marsh separating the highland from the shore line. It was a long and hard walk, but we made it countless times. It was usually harder going back because we always had a potato sack of mallards, black ducks, widgeon, or teal to carry.

When the weather was bad, it was rough going through the black needlegrass and mud. The journey from the Bay shore to the comparative shelter of the pine woods surrounding the Cowhole could be dangerous in fog or snow.

Once in winter, three of us had been poaching ducks in the Bay shore ponds when the weather turned bad. A northwest snow storm blew in unexpectedly, and we decided that we should head for shelter. We were young and in good shape, but as the snow got deeper it became a real effort to walk in the mud and grass. Finally one of my companions, Gene Crockett, got to the point that he simply could not walk any longer, even though I was carrying his gun. There was nothing to do but carry him out of The Marsh, so he climbed onto my back and our companion carried our arsenal. After awhile, when he began to tire too, I added the three shotguns to my load and we kept on going.

The snow got thicker, the mud got thinner, the needlegrass got thicker and I got more tired. It was a struggle to keep on. I began to ponder our fate. If I gave out, I would have to decide whether to leave my friend or the guns behind, a true dilemma, but to be honest, I think I was leaning to the guns. Fortunately, it did not come to that, and soon we were in the comparative shelter of the pines and the ground was firmer.

I suppose I did the proper thing in carrying my companion out of The Marsh. He is now a prominent local banker and gives me five percent on my savings and charges me only ten percent on my mortgages.

The other companion was my cousin, Melvin, the anchor man on the half-mile relay team. He was much swifter barefoot on a gravel track than in gum boots* on a marsh.

Then there was a later occasion when another fellow poacher and I encountered a different type of problem when the weather was beautiful. Actually, you may say the weather caused the problem.

The local rural mail carrier, the father of my friend Hall Ames, would leave Hall and me off within striking distance of The Marsh and its duck ponds in the course of his duty. One day, we easily gained access to the Bay shore after crossing the vast expanse of needlegrass and mud. We had a good shoot and bagged a variety of waterfowl that morning. Sitting on the sand dunes after lunch, we decided to take a nap, warmed by the bright sun. We dozed away, and after awhile we were awakened by noises and sat up just as two adult duck hunters walked up to us. One man appeared to be in authority and he politely asked our names. His name was Buck Comstock and he was leasing The Marsh for hunting from his companion Franklin Lewis, who was the current owner. They did not have to ask what we were doing. This was apparent from the pile of ducks beside us.

I fully expected to be hauled off to jail and was surprised when Mr. Comstock said, "Well, one of you boys come with me and one can go with Mr. Lewis and we'll shoot some more ducks." This was an offer that was hard to refuse, but we were so embarrassed we declined, saying that it was time to go. Mr. Comstock politely asked us to let him know when we wanted to go duck hunting again. He later pur-

* Black rubber boots that come to the hips.

chased this natural paradise from Mr. Lewis and enjoyed it for many years until his death. He was a gentleman.

Prior to Lewis' ownership, this property was owned by Captain Jack Melson and thus its name of Melson's Marsh. I have always thought of it with this appellation.

Captain Jack, who never owned a boat larger than twenty feet, and who was never in the military, made his living from the land and the water. He farmed in the crop season and trapped ducks and sold oysters the rest of the year. Early in the century trapping ducks became illegal, but it was a long time before Captain Jack became very concerned about that. However, one day when he was at the grocery store in town socializing with some of his cronies, a stranger walked in. Of course, a hush fell over the group of farmers, fishermen and hunters gathered around the big pot-bellied stove. The stranger began to ask a few questions about land for sale. He seemed like a nice enough fellow, so gradually the air thawed and everybody became friendly. Somehow the conversation turned to ducks, and the stranger let on as to how he would like to buy some black ducks.

Captain Jack, either feeling compassion for the man's needs or his own, or probably both, invited him to come home with him for a wild duck dinner and a little commerce. The stranger accepted and followed his new friend down the neck to the Melson home, where he was warmly welcomed, customary in those days. While Mrs. Melson was making preparations for dinner, the stranger went with Captain Jack to his duck trap to gather up a few corn-fed black ducks and mallards. Some were for selling and some for eating that evening.

The stranger had a hardy meal, and all of the Melsons took a liking to him, for the time being. After dinner he was entertained with stories of duck trapping, baiting and shooting, and appeared to be genuinely amused. Then came the time for good-bye, and the stranger took a book out of his pocket and gave Captain Jack a summons for trapping ducks. The only problem with any of this was the chronology; knowing the people of the area and the times, he could have given Captain Jack the ticket before dinner and everyone would still have had a pleasant meal and parted friends because the stranger was a likable fellow. It is just as much a crime to waste friendship as ducks.

No mention of The Marsh would be complete without a little information on the Yahoo that inhabited the area. There is no better way to describe it than in Captain Jack's own words. He dictated the following to Mary Easley in 1957, when he was an old man. She was as honest and true an old maid as ever lived, and Captain Jack never lied.

The Story of the Yahoo
by Captain Jack Melson
February 16, 1957

It was the greatest thing ever came across me! I was going across the marsh one day. I was driving a horse cart. When I got over there, I heard a peculiar noise. Sounded like someone driving a pole in the water. Thought it was Captain Fred Harrison, but further I got down there, the noise was further to my left. I came to the conclusion it was not Captain Fred so I kept on down. When I got to the Bay shore, I stopped the horse and the fuss was coming out the marsh. I listened to it and could not tell to save my life what it was, and I have never known what it was. I drove on to where the noise was and then it stopped. This was the first time I ever heard it, probably 35 years ago.

Then, you could hear it most every year, and I never could find out what it was. Sometime you would think it was one thing. Thought it could be a muskrat but never heard it where other muskrats or other animals were, and I never heard it anywhere else.

On one occasion, Omar Kellam and I went down and we heard the sound or fuss calling in the marsh. I said, "Let's go and see if we can find that thing." So I got out close to the noise, close as to that puppy (which was under his feet). I looked with all my eyes and I had my gun with me, and I shot right where I heard the noise and it shut right up. I never heard it any more.

It has a funny sound. Has about three different sounds to it. Had some funny experiences with the thing. One time I wanted to go somewhere, and I sent Johnnie on the marsh for something. Always heard it in the spring or summer, March to July. Johnnie went out there, and he heard that thing and he almost ran his toenails off. Ewell heard it, too, and thought it would scare Johnnie and went to get him. I have not heard it for at least ten years.

Bobby Melson, grandson, says at a distance the sound is like someone driving a fish pole in water, but near it has three distinct chirps, then goes back to sounding like a pole being driven. Says grandfather is getting deaf. Has not heard it for ages but has not been down to look for it.

Many reliable, sober-minded oldtimers had heard the Yahoo, people whose veracity was never questioned, nor should it have been. An example of this was Ewell Melson, son of Captain Jack, who owned The Marsh and the old 1780 home on some high land near The Marsh's southern edge. Ewell was born and raised there and was always a great outdoorsman. He spent a lot of his time shooting ducks and trapping raccoons and muskrats around the ponds and creek shores and probably knew The Marsh as well as any man. But he also was the salt of the earth when it came to honesty, sanity and all of those attributes which made him the kind of person you must believe if you would believe anyone.

The tale he told me one day when I stopped by his home to buy some peeler crabs always comes to my mind if the sun sets on me on The Marsh. Ewell and his brother, Johnny, had been shooting black ducks one evening and had started back home. With about a mile to go, it was getting dark. As they walked through The Marsh they heard the Yahoo giving its weird call, so they quickened the pace. The Yahoo, however, got closer and closer until it seemed to be right on their heels. They could neither see nor hear anything except the repeated cries of the Yahoo. Ewell said the sound appeared to be coming out of the footprints left in the mud. Finally, in desperation, he fired his shotgun down into the mud almost at his heels. At this point the noise stopped and they continued on home. He also tells of hearing it on many other occasions. But it always kept its distance after this instance.

In the ensuing years, I have been back to The Marsh many times under more legal circumstances to hunt waterfowl. In the spring I go just to watch the birds and stroll the three-mile beach on the Bay.

I have grown to love this spot about as much as any other that I had ever seen on earth. Just recently our sculpture company purchased it from the heirs of the generous Mr. Comstock. It will not be so bad to depart this crowded world, knowing that my children, grandchildren, and hopefully their children will have a place to hide from the masses and play with nature.

To bring everything full circle, I will tell you about a recent expedition to The Marsh with my first grandson, Jason, a couple of years ago when he was about nine. Although I do not like to shoot ducks anymore and I have some reservations about encouraging my grandson to do so, I wanted him to bag at least one duck in the area where I had so many wonderful experiences. I wanted him to have at least a fleeting glimpse of an era that will never return.

On a cold, windy day, I bought him a pair of hipboots and he and I traveled by boat along the Bay shore to our solar cottage, in the exact spot where Hall Ames and I were soaking up the sun about forty-five years ago when Mr. Comstock walked up to us and our pile of poached ducks.

After final preparations, we started walking along the area between the Bay shore and the ponds and marsh, looking for ducks. Because of an unusual cold spell, there was a lot of ice on the ponds and a slush of it along the shore. We saw a couple of ducks and were attempting to creep up on them when they jumped out of range. Because our prey had escaped, I stood up. An entire flock, which we had not previously seen, jumped, so we, or rather I, who was in command, had messed up.

We continued our duck expedition and soon saw a flock sitting on the Bay shore. Creeping through the grass behind the dunes, we began a long stalk. We crawled far and it was cold. Occasionally, I peeped over the dunes to see what kind of progress we were making. Then we crawled some more. The prospect of Jason's getting a shot at a drake mallard looked good, so we continued. Finally, we were almost upon the unsuspecting ducks. I was very proud of showing my grandson how to creep up on ducks, an important art in bygone days, but possibly not a prerequisite to blissful living in today's world.

I remembered the days when flocks of waterfowl covered this beautiful marsh, and I kept many families partially fed and had great fun doing so. Now, after the long crawl, it looked as though my grandson would get a chance with his little twenty-gauge single-shot gun to have a shot at a duck. We hunkered down to crawl a little farther and still had good cover. The thirty miles per hour northwest wind was in our faces and we could not be heard over the sound of the waves on the shore. We were almost to the point where Jason could try his luck when all of the ducks suddenly rose into the air and escaped. I was a little embarrassed but didn't really think I had done anything wrong. Still, I was puzzled. One of the disadvantages of going past middle age is that when you err it then takes awhile to figure out why. At least in this case it was not my fault. As we stood to watch our fat mallard meal disappear somewhere toward Baltimore, the culprit appeared. It was a bald eagle cruising the shoreline, looking for a duck meal, just as we were. We all were disappointed.

I consoled my grandson and told him that I knew of a special pond which always had a few ducks swimming around in it and that we would go by it on the way home. I was certain we would have better luck there. It was not too far to this pond of about an acre; the cover was good and the going was easy. As we approached, we kept behind some thick saltwater bushes, not even attempting to see if it were inhabited until we were in striking distance. At the proper point and behind the same ancient bayberry and cedar bushes which many years ago covered my approach, I called a halt to the stalk to reconnoiter the area; and there they were, two ducks, hooded mergansers, swimming unsuspectingly in good range for Jason's diminutive twenty-gauge. Along with the ducks were about five pied-billed grebes or water witches, as they are locally called. Of course, they are not good to eat and are not game birds and they were of no consequence, or at least so I thought at the time.

Anyway, I gave Jason some last minute instructions and told him to stand up slowly and take a shot. He stood up, cocked his gun, slowly raised it and aimed at the ducks. Jason seemed hesitant and a little nervous. He lowered his gun and kept on looking at his prey. He raised his gun again and took aim as I waited for the report of his twenty-gauge. Again he lowered his gun and turned to me and said, "Granddad, I don't feel good." So we turned and walked back toward our boat, anchored along the shore of the Chesapeake.

You see, grebes are little birds and mergansers are much bigger but they both eat minnows and are frequently found together. It was clear what Jason meant when he complained of not feeling good when he later said, "Granddad, I didn't know ducks had babies in the winter."

EPILOGUE

As I write this, I am looking at the sun setting over the Chesapeake. There is a transient green flash, a little reminder of my own life in this area.

Before me lies that mysterious marsh, the same one my cousin Melvin and I timidly explored fifty years ago. I now own this piece of land on which I consistently poached for twenty years. The tide is ebbing and the rails call frequently as I listen expectantly for the Yahoo, which I have never heard.

Through my binoculars, I can see black ducks settling into the ponds along the Bay shore about a mile or two away. Some duck species seem to like it here and nest on The Marsh rather than migrate north.

From the vantage point of my lookout tower, I can see the area where my companion, Hall Ames, and I were dozing in the sand dunes after a successful morning shooting ducks when the owner caught us. I now have a small cottage on this spot.

I can see the general area of the trek I took across The Marsh with my future banker, Gene Crockett, on my back during a snowstorm with Melvin trailing along.

The tide is ebbing and the prow of an old log canoe gradually comes above the surface of the water. It has been there for a century or so, but it is made of heart pine which was mature before Columbus sailed west. It will endure another ten thousand tides. There is no heart pine left now except the secondhand variety from old homes and barns, just yellow second-growth sapwood, which at one time was used for nothing better than pigpens.

A few isolated oysters come into view in Back Creek. They are almost gone now. Not so long ago you could walk on them for miles without muddying your boots.

Along the edge of the Bay a group of pelicans wings its way to an unknown roosting place. They, too, were not present when I was young. Some things learn to live with man and survive, some do not. Others are cyclic. The pelicans come here every summer now but were unknown to my father. Yet I read in the local newspaper column, Yester-years, an article from a century ago which said, "the pelicans have gone south for the winter".

I try to envision lines of Indians walking single-file across this vast marsh. I know that they walked single-file because that's the way Melvin and I, and our friends walked. It just seems natural. There is much evidence of the Indian presence: huge piles of thousand-year-old oyster shells, arrowheads and clay basket fragments.

Life, it seems, is a combination of cycles and dead ends. The Indians, the real owners of this pristine wilderness, are the ultimate example of the latter. The ducks are disappearing. In the 1950's, when I hunted with Mitt and Cabell, they frequently complained about the demise of waterfowl, even though to me it seemed as though the world was full of ducks. I imagine that my grandson, Jason, thought the same way when I told him how it was when I was his age. Perhaps he will someday tell his child or grandchild about how many birds there were when he and I tried to bag a duck. If it is true that everything in nature is relative, it is also true that it is mostly downhill.

But the exception is the two whitetail bucks I can see jostling in the distance near the wild hibiscus where the Loblolly pines meet the spartina and needlegrass of The Marsh. I would estimate that there are now two hundred whitetails on this twelve hundred acre property. Only twenty years or so ago there were none. These fleet, elusive, beautiful animals have gradually worked their way south from Maryland. I believe two main factors are responsible for this:

the increased plantings of soybeans, which they love, and the increase in the cutover timberland which affords cover and food. Just two hundred years ago deer were already extinct in this area. Now they are omnipresent.

The Indians will not return, the deer and pelicans have, the fate of the oysters and black mallards is still in the wind.

I have gone from trespasser to owner of this paradise. And while my dreams and future frame of mind depend on this land, I know that the comfort of the twilight will never compare to the thrill of the uncertain dawn.

> *"It is not writing that I like, it is having written."*
> *Ernest Hemingway*

MARYLAND PAPERBACK BOOKSHELF

Also of Interest in the Series:

The Oyster: A Popular Summary of a Scientific Study,
   by William K. Brooks

The Lord's Oysters, by Gilbert Byron

Home on the Canal, by Elizabeth Kytle

Happy Days: 1880–1892, by H. L. Mencken

Watermen, by Randall S. Peffer

Young Frederick Douglass: The Maryland Years,
   by Dickson J. Preston